May th[...] inspire you to discover breakthrough lessons from your own life!

Pamela Elaine

MW00948835

Destined for Greatness Enterprises, Inc.
P.O. Box 167
Bala Cynwyd, PA 19004
215-395-6043
www.MyMuddyHighHeels.com

All rights reserved. No part of this book may be reproduced, scanned, or distributed in any printed or electronic form without written permission from the author. Please do not participate in or encourage piracy of copyrighted materials in violation of the author's rights. Purchase only authorized editions.

Grateful acknowledgment is made for permission to reprint excerpts and quotes from authors as cited in the Appendix.

Copyright © 2014 by Pamela Elaine Nichols
All rights reserved.
ISBN-13: 978-1500924799
ISBN-10: 1500924792

Book Designed by DionaNicole Design Studio, LLC
150 Monument Road, Suite 207, PMB# 0038
Bala Cynwyd, Pennsylvania 19004
www.dionanicole.com

Cover Design: Diona Murray
Interior Design: Brent Bush

DEDICATIONS

To my mother, Vertia B Walker Wright, who showed me through her life's example what a woman's strength really is.

***

To Taylor Raye, Alonzo James, Wynter Elaine and Kendall Lillian Jaye. You make my life perfect!

***

To CBJ for the gift of your commitment for 18 years and devotion to our children.

***

To every woman who wants to take care of the mother who lives inside of her.

EDITOR'S NOTE

At the time Pamela Elaine asked me to edit her book, I was experiencing a very difficult period in my life. My mother had recently passed, and as a certified momma's boy, I was devastated. Because I never knew my dad, my mom was my world. To compound matters, my baby, my youngest son, suddenly and unexpectedly moved to Florida with my ex-wife. I had never felt such emptiness, such a feeling of loss. My circumstance changed from seeing and spending quality time with my son on a regular basis, to not seeing him for months at a time.

Reading about Pamela Elaine's life and her very personal, intimate experiences helped me to better understand myself and pinpoint the fact that I was suffering from depression and major self-esteem issues. She helped give me the courage to seek professional counseling to help me deal with my overwhelming sense of loss and my diminished sense of self. Pamela Elaine's journal and my therapist helped me to understand that as a full-time single dad with two extraordinary young men, I neglected to place value on my own needs for far too long.

My testimony is this: When my youngest son moved from Maryland to Florida, months at a time would pass before I was able to see him. I had never felt such pain, that is, until my mom passed. I tried to take control of the situation by arguing with my ex-wife, imploring her not to move, and petitioning the courts to enforce my rights as a father, all to no avail. I was angry, depressed, hurt, and frustrated.

As I read Pamela Elaine's life-lesson on surrender, something resonated within me. It helped me to understand and admit that I truly wasn't in control. With the help of a great therapist, amazing family and friends, my oldest son, Christopher, and Pamela Elaine's insightful life-lessons, I learned to surrender my perceived control of the situation with my son. I'm learning daily to forgive myself, my ex-wife, and others that I've resented. I began to let go of the anger, the pain, and the frustration. Letting go of the anger and resentment allowed me to open my mind to the fact that everything happens for a reason, even when I don't understand nor agree with that reason.

I finally admitted to myself: "I can't take it anymore….and I surrender!" (Pamela Elaine's Lesson #3). As soon as I admitted this, I began to feel lighter, as though a great weight had been lifted. For the first time in quite a while, I began to feel joy. Subsequently, I began to implement Pamela Elaine's other life-lesson (#8) on a daily basis, which is to "intend joy." Within a week of my surrender, my ex-wife phoned to inform me that they were moving from Florida and would be living much closer to me. She also informed me that I would be able to see him on a much more regular basis than I was able to when they were in Florida.

I've been telling Pamela Elaine for many months that her life-lessons are also relevant to men, especially fathers. My hope is that many lives will be transformed as a result of reading these life-lessons, including men and single fathers.

Pamela Elaine, thank you for your courage and honesty. It has made a difference in my life!

- Dana Edward Lintz, M.ED.

TABLE OF CONTENTS

TABLE OF CONTENTS (CONT.)

ACKNOWLEDGEMENTS

This book has been inside of me for decades. Getting it from the inside onto paper was laborious. A lot of thought was put into the decision to be transparent about my life and the lessons it has taught me. This was a difficult decision for me. That's why I could not have written this book without the support and kindness of many "Book Angels." I would have nothing to write if not for the lessons learned from people who have come into my life.

Book Angels
I am indebted to my editor, Dana Lintz, who held sacred my story. From his editing of my life lessons, I think he may be the only man who knows me intimately. When I wanted to quit writing and abandon the project altogether, Dana encouraged me (well, threatened really!) to keep writing because there are many mothers (and fathers, he emphatically pointed out) who will benefit from this book.

I am grateful to my reviewers, Cheryl Hurley and Phyllis Hicks, for their insightful contributions and challenging questions that improved the book's story. I give deep thanks to Phyllis for rescuing me during my breakdown, a topic of this book.

My gratitude is extended to Donna Hergenroeder for encouraging me to submit my story to The Dr. Oz Show. Because of her encouragement, I had the honor of being one of Dr. Oz's guests.

Thanks to Cathy Coleman for coaching me from fat to fabulous!

Celeste De Bease showed me that swimming in the river is freeing. I am deeply grateful to her and to Sabrina Beckham, my SheROX Triathlon river coach, for inspiring me to make peace with the river. I could not have finished the SheROX Triathlon swim without the help of my unknown Angel who came to my aid in the moment I needed it most. I don't know her name or who she is. Perhaps I never will.

My father, Ernest James Nichols, has my deepest respect because he showed me that a life can heal and a heart can change. He is my Daddy and my best friend.

I am grateful to Dr. Margaret Bass for taking a risk to be straight with me about my personal struggle and for encouraging me to seek professional help. And, to Debra Good for giving me that professional help.

I acknowledge Susan Tabor-Kleiman for introducing me to a program that taught me breakthrough technology to live a life I now love.

Thank you to Sherry Levesque, my Transcendental Meditation Teacher, who gave me my mantra; my anchor friend, Nicole O'Neal, for praying with me at a pivotal junction in my life; my financial advisor, Rob Shangraw, for getting me on a path to wealth; Boris Mack for poignant words that made my choice for graduate school easy; Deborah Pegues for introducing me to the book that showed me how to live with purpose; and, John Murray, who encouraged me to write a book, even suggesting what the opening chapter should be.

I am eternally indebted to my two other anchor friends, Brita DeBrest and Donna Gholar, for keeping me grounded and holding me close as I walked through the dark tunnel of divorce.

My step-father, The Reverend Dr. Thomas Wright, who loves me unconditionally. I am honored to be your daughter and relish in your support.

Muddy High Heels

A Journey and a Journal

Pamela Elaine Nichols

FOREWORD

Pamela Elaine Nichols is a venerable giant in the field of women's health, enlightening us over the years regarding the need for physical, emotional, and spiritual wellness. A powerful leader, she has been a personal friend and colleague for many years. I am delighted to have been given the privilege of sharing this journey with Pamela Elaine. I have enjoyed watching as she has helped women from various walks of life move from devastation to destiny. Through workshops, seminars, various speaking engagements, and her recent appearance on the Dr. Oz show, she has been an example of resilience and the embodiment of the power of a positive and healthy transition out of difficult situations for women across the nation. Through her authenticity, many are discovering that they are destined for greatness.

Muddy High Heels is a treasure for women (especially mothers) and the men who love them. Integrating the stories from her own life, she draws upon 14 powerful life lessons to provide insights that touch the mind, soul, and spirit.

Women of all ages will find this book insightful as the author invites them on a real life journey into the "mysterious and elusive" place called destiny; but not before unlocking a painful truth of a childhood marred with the pain of an adulterous father and the betrayal which threatened to render her powerless and broken.

Truly a treasure of truth, freedom hovers over the person who will read each chapter with an open and receptive heart. Mothers will discover themselves within the pages of this book. For the person looking forward to a life free from emotional isolation, Pamela Elaine unlocks her own doors of disappointment and provides keys for the rest of us to do the same.

Muddy High Heels is a must read for any mother who has ever found herself at the point of giving up. If you have ever said, "I can't take it anymore," you will find the strength you need to recover from your breakdown or breakup. You will break through as you realize a greater, more powerful reality invites you.

As you travel to the depths of despair with the author, and perhaps find yourself crouched on the bathroom floor sobbing uncontrollably, or in the middle of a divorce after many years, each chapter of this book provides a consistent reminder that, "weeping may endure for a night, but joy comes in the morning." From Lesson 1 through 14, Muddy High Heels will leave you speechless as you take the journey with the author and discover ways to address concerns, such as, betrayal, abandonment, depression, isolation, and rejection.

For every mother who has ever felt like giving up, for every spouse or significant family member who has felt the pain and powerlessness of watching a love one suffer from the debilitating effects of depression, and for every person who has been desperate to find a path leading to your destiny, Muddy High Heels is for you.

As a counselor, marriage and family doctoral candidate, and mother, I resonate with the author. What a wonderful gift this book is. As you read through its pages, I am sure you will echo the beautiful sentiments of Pamela Elaine when she says: "These lessons enabled me to transform pain into purpose, hurt into healing, tears into triumph, regret into resilience, and depression into destiny."

So let your journey begin!

Cathy R. Coleman, M.H.S.

(Cathy is author of Treasures of the Heart, *a poetry journal that inspires men and women to live their best life now. A researcher and student, she is currently working on a doctorate in Marriage and Family Counseling.)*

"There is an eagle in me that wants to soar, and there is a hippopotamus in me that wants to wallow in the mud."

- Carl Sanburg

INTRODUCTION

I Wrote This Journal for Every Mother Who Has Lost Herself

Muddy High Heels is a journal of 14 life-lessons I learned while digging myself out of the mud of a breakdown and a breakup. I share my deepest and most shameful moments I experienced while in this mud. These experiences were difficult, some messy, and others just plain ugly. However, from each experience, a lesson emerged that was brilliant, sophisticated, and sexy, just like red high-heel shoes. Each lesson I share with you is one that I learned over time. I still practice these lessons today. Practicing these lessons (and many more I promise to share with you in future editions) has made my life meaningful and rich.

These lessons have enabled me to transform my pain into purpose, hurt into healing, tears into triumph, regret into resilience, and depression into destiny. As you will read, I lost myself in the noble work of being mother and wife. Perhaps, one might argue, I never possessed the "Who" of who I was in the first place. In order to lose something, you have to first have it. There may be truth to this argument. Regardless of whom I **thought** I was, I got lost in the busyness of caring for four children and being a wife to a good man. While everyone else's needs were my priority, I ignored my own. Ignoring my own needs proved a costly mistake for those I love and for me.

As mothers, most of us desire growth and personal fulfillment, but not at the expense of the wellness of those we love. We love our children and want the best for them, and we want to be the ones who provide what's best. However, we are torn between fulfilling the needs of others and meeting our own. In other words, we are constantly caught in the proverbial "work-life balance" vortex. Most of the time, the needs of those we care for take precedence over our own, and we are left feeling as if we have lost something, somewhere, somehow.

What I lost was myself, and what I found was years of unhappiness, frustration, and longing. But, you would never have known. During those years, I walked, talked, and behaved like a woman who seemed to have it all together. Yet inside, I was falling apart, resenting almost every moment of being who and where I was. Worst of all, I felt completely alone. Everyone else around me seemed to be managing her roles. Mothers I knew—both closely and not so closely – did not appear to be caught up in the vortex like I was, or so it seemed. Of course, I heard occasional complaints about the challenges of being a wife and mother. But their complaints were usually accompanied by a few chuckles and then a return to the routine of cooking, cleaning, chauffeuring, yada, yada, yada. Tears and tantrums followed none of their complaints like they followed mine, and I kept mine a secret. Not wanting to be odd-woman out, I kept my pain and discontent locked inside a closet.

After an unforgettable bathroom floor-crying episode (okay, break-down), I committed to finding a symbiotic relationship between caring for the needs of others and caring for mine too. I found my path and set out on a long journey. That journey revealed some simple--and also difficult--lessons. However, I didn't care about how easy or difficult the lessons. My only concern was that I remain open to the God of the Universe to lead me out of my current place and into a place I longed to be: a place I call Destiny.

Muddy High Heels is both the title of my journey and a journal of my life-lessons. It is still, however, a work in progress, as am I. I began writing these lessons as emails to myself. Whenever it dawned on me that God was teaching me a lesson (whether or not I applied it immediately), I sloppily converted it into an email addressed to myself. These lessons would manifest as "ah-ha" moments. For example, while taking a shower or drying a load of clothes, a lesson would bombard my mind. Other times, the lesson came slowly, methodically, as I asked the God of the Universe for the meaning behind the pain or frustration. As I mentioned, some lessons were quite obvious (like, "duhhhh"), while others were more difficult ("Leave me alone, God. I'll get back to you in a year or two."). Whether simple or difficult, each lesson lightened my burden, opened my mind, and transformed my heart and life. Over time, I compiled 75 life-lessons! I offer only 14 of those lessons at this time, but there are more to come in subsequent editions.

***

This journal is dedicated to the wellness and happiness of all the mothers of the world. We are remarkable creations--divinely designed to give birth and to be everything to others. To others, our wellness may not seem like it matters. BUT...OUR WELLNESS DOES MATTER! Some 82.5 million mothers make 85% of household spending decisions, contribute $2 trillion in buying power, give birth to 100% of the population, yet dedicate very little time to our wellness and happiness.

My prayer is this: As you read these lessons, you will find one or two that speak to you in an "ah-ha" way, and that you will apply those lessons to your own life. Since this is a journal, you can write down your "ah-ha moments," and reflect on them over time. I encourage you to formulate your own life-lessons too, and share them with others. Ultimately, I hope these lessons inspire you to become who you truly are: a mother who has the power to turn any mess into something beautiful, much like red high-heel shoes.

Welcome to the Journey. Keep learning. Keep growing. Keep living. Keep loving!

- Pamela Elaine

HOW THIS JOURNEY AND JOURNAL WORK

This is a journal of 14 life-lessons, and it is our journey together. The format of the journey and journal is as follows:

- Statement of the lesson learned
- My personal story of how the lesson manifested
- Application of the lesson to your life
- A journal question/challenge with pages for you to write your reflections, thoughts, and insight about how the lesson applies to your life.

At the end of this journal, you can record your top life-lessons. Also, I invite you to write to me and share a lesson or two. We can continue an exchange of lessons learned, because sharing lessons and learning from one another adds to a rich and enjoyable life.

You can write to me at Thanks@DFGreatness.com

A NOTE ABOUT THE PLACE CALLED DESTINY

In 2001, Linda Brown, Shelly Pullian, Cheryl Hurley, Cheryl Nichols and I sat around my piano and co-wrote the lyrics to the song, "Woman of Destiny". One of the women had previously begun writing these lyrics. Long before co-writing the song, I personally yearned to be a woman of "destiny," though I wasn't quite sure what "destiny" meant for me. The manner in which I described myself at that point in my life in no way included the term, "destiny." In retrospect, what I really longed for was a clear path toward destiny. That path was unknown, but I believed it existed. Through the application of life-lessons, I would have to travel that path with a willing foot, a courageous gait, and a flexible pace.

"Destiny" is an abstract word that is mysterious and elusive. A definition from Merriam Webster is, ***"the power or agency that determines the course of events."*** Who or what is this "power/agency?" And what course of events are we talking about? Good course? Bad course? Neutral course? And, if this "power" has already determined the course of [your] events, then what in the heck do you need to do, other than submit? It seems we have no control when it comes to destiny.

All of us have experienced the mysterious and elusive events of destiny. And during these experiences, we felt we had no control. Not having control may be factual. However, I believe we do have some control that may not be recognized immediately in this definition. It's hidden. Hidden within this definition is choice. We have five possible choices: 1) **Who** we want to become; 2) **What** we do with our time; 3) **When** we surrender our will to a Divine will; 4) **Where** we invest our gifts and talents; and, 5) **How** we respond to our circumstances. These five possibilities shape a woman of destiny.

The woman of destiny that I longed to be was one who: 1) loves herself and others wholeheartedly, courageously, and confidently; 2) spends her time making a difference in the lives of others; 3) consults the wisdom and direction of her God continuously; 4) invests her gifts and talents into the lives of women who have the noble task of raising children.

After being a mother for fourteen years, being married and divorced twice, and learning and continually practicing these life-lessons, I can now declare that I am, finally, a Woman of Destiny!

I share these life-lessons with the hope that they might help shape and define the woman you desire to be, whether you already know that woman, or have no idea who she is. Perhaps these life-lessons will help you circumvent unnecessary mistakes and fast-forward you to your desired destination. Think about it. If you want to get to the Caribbean, wouldn't you rather spend as little time getting there as possible and as much time being there as possible? Certainly, you can take as much time as you want getting there. Your path need not be direct. It can be circuitous. Just consider the cost of a direct route, as compared to a circuitous one. Then decide.

I invite you to define your destiny and to marvel at who you become.

NOW, IT'S TIME TO SHARE MY TRUTH

"... Know the truth, and the truth will make you free"

- The Gospel of John 8:32

The truth is freeing, and here is my truth: I never wanted to be a mom. And as a mom, I felt depleted. I was resentful. I felt alone, guilty, incompetent, trapped, and ashamed. I never wanted to be a mom for one basic reason: I did not want to soil the precious lives of my children with personal baggage that I hadn't yet unpacked. The seemingly endless, daily task of taking responsibility for four other young, innocent lives was often unbearable. The burden of being the primary person upon whom they depended was frightening most of the time. Honestly, I was not prepared to raise children because I still felt like a hurt child myself.

But who feels free to reveal this truth, especially to other mothers? Who feels free to admit that she's miserable being a mom? After all, moms are supposed to love their role, and give of themselves tirelessly, without complaint, right? Well, I certainly didn't love it, and I complained to myself all the time. And yet, all the while I pretended that everything was okay and that I was happy.

"What was the turning point?" In 2007, seven years prior to writing this book, the pretense came to a screeching halt. I had a breakdown on my bathroom floor. I locked myself in the bathroom, but my four children still heard my sobbing. They banged on the door, begging me to open it. I refused. I wouldn't even open it for my husband. I knew I had to make a change. I had to find a way to turn an unfulfilling job, which I never wanted, into one that had meaning and fulfillment.

And I did! I figured it out!

Ironically, my children helped me figure out what I needed to do to find happiness and fulfillment as a woman and mother. They taught me many of the lessons I share in the coming pages. One profound lesson was that fulfillment--in all aspects of life--begins by looking inward. It begins within me!

My hope is to inspire you to create health and happiness in the one key relationship that is often overlooked: with yourself. When you step into your creative power, you will experience breakthroughs in your relationships with your children, partner, co-workers, and members of your community. I stand by this statement!

I stepped into my creative power, and while my relationship with my children and others is much better, I still have work to do. However, my relationship with myself is finally healthy and strong.

While this truth was difficult, facing it was a prerequisite in the course called, "A Life Worth Living."

Muddy High Heels Theme Song

Written by Pamela Elaine and Lynda Staton
© February 2014

A master of disguise
Masking what was true
No one knew I was drowning
So what could they do?
Had to be my own hero
Putting my life on the line
Couldn't even save myself
But, His grace would come in time

It's not that I didn't love my family
Was a choice I gladly made
Had no idea with all the choosing
I'd lose myself along the way
The beautiful struggle being a mother
With all the sacrifices it brought
Ironic it was my babies
Who pulled me out of the rut

Stepping out from the shadows
I was able to clearly see
That the place that held me back
Was deep inside of me

The
Breakdown

"Someday I will find my prince, but my Daddy will always be my King."

- Pamela Elaine

LESSON

1

You Are Fearfully And Wonderfully Made[1].

Tall, dark, and handsome, he was the apple of my eye. I loved and adored Daddy. I can recall on at least two occasions sitting in his lap and rubbing my soft cheek against his rough, prickly beard. It didn't matter that my cheeks got a little scratched. The sheer pleasure of being so close to him made every scratch worthwhile.

In my early years, Daddy was a very present figure. I remember vacations across the country in the car together with Daddy, Mommy, my sister, and my brother. Daddy would talk to me about the historical sites, about God, and about being special because I was the youngest. I remember at about the age of four, I flew to Dallas, Texas with Daddy to visit his mother. It was a last minute decision, so Mommy didn't have time to comb my hair. Daddy had to do it for the first time! When we met Grandmother at the airport, she was horrified at the mess my father made of my hair! Using her fingers as the comb and her hands as the brush, she quickly fixed my hair. But it didn't matter. I was traveling, alone, with Daddy. How special he made me feel!

During the early Jackson 5 era, every parent looked to find talent in his own child. Was it possible that Daddy's three children might be the next Jackson 5? After quickly discovering that I had musical and acting talents, he signed me up with an advertising agency in Los Angeles. I earned a little money as a model for magazines. But that wasn't the exciting part. In fact, it was a bit boring standing around waiting, then more standing around just posing, and then more standing around waiting. What was exciting was being called over the school intercom to be dismissed from class because Daddy was waiting in the principal's office to take ME to MY next modeling session. I tried to control my excitement as I gathered my books and waved "good-bye" to my classmates. I wasn't nearly as excited about another modeling session as I was about spending time alone, again, with Daddy. How special he made me feel!

Not only did Daddy make me feel special, he was also my HERO! The day Daddy became my hero is a day I will never forget. My sister, brother, and I went on a fishing trip off a pier in Los Angeles with Mommy and Daddy. Fascinated by the fish below, I reached into the ocean to touch one. As I bent down, I tumbled right into the water—head first. I started sinking. I looked up and could see my sister perched on the edge of the pier reaching out her hand to grab me. I couldn't reach her; I just couldn't reach her! I was sinking faster and faster it seemed. Suddenly, as quickly as I fell in, I was pulled up and out of the water and back onto the pier. My sister saved me! Mommy quickly dried me off, packed our bags, and put us in the car. During the ride home, I repeatedly thanked my sister for saving my life. Daddy and Mommy were very quiet during the drive home, troubled by the close call of losing their youngest child. When we got home, I wanted to reward my sister for her bravery, so I gave her all of the money in my piggy bank. She took the money, started walking out of the room, and then slowly turned to confess:

"Pam... I...I didn't pull you out of the ocean. Daddy did."

"Daddy did? But it was your hand I saw reaching out to me. I grabbed your hand, not Daddy's."

"I held your hand tight", she corrected. "But Daddy jumped in the water and got you out."

Slowly, reluctantly she gave back my $5.76.

Thankfully, my sister held onto my hand to keep me from drifting away. That way, Daddy could save my life. MY Daddy saved MY life!?! Daddy risked his own life to save mine? Yet, he said nothing about it. The whole ride home, as I lavished praise and thanks upon my sister, he was quiet. He let me believe it was my sister – rather than him - who saved me. Daddy was my beloved and I was his. How special he made me feel!

Then one day, Daddy stopped being my Hero. I remember exactly when it happened. Around the age of ten, Daddy stopped being around as much. We didn't spend time together like before. The modeling calls stopped. Subsequent trips to Texas to see his mother were trips I took without him.

"Hi, Daddy. Where you going today, Daddy? Can we-?"

"I gotta go to work." He'd interrupt. "I'll be back after 'while.'"

And out the door he would go, quickly, without looking at me. One day...two days...sometimes three days would pass...then he'd come through the door early in the morning or late in the evening. I was so happy to see him. It didn't matter that he had been gone for days. He was home now.

"Hi Daddy. Where you going today?" But he'd be in a bad mood, so he wouldn't say much. He'd go to his room, close the door, get in bed, and go to sleep.

On a good day, when he was around, he'd talk to me a little. He had no idea how his few words were filled with great meaning for me. Attempting to be affectionate, sometimes he would call me "little ole ugly girl." He called me this enough times that I started to believe him. I took "little ole ugly girl" with me everywhere I went. I compared my looks to those of my peers. I didn't look like them. They were beautiful with light skin and long hair. I was ugly with dark skin and nappy hair. I compared my looks to other girls' on a daily basis. My self-esteem began to drop like mercury in a thermometer. It hit its lowest the day I learned a terrible truth.

Mommy had been suspicious that Daddy might be having an affair with another woman. Huh? Mommy had dreams. She saw things. Somehow, she found an unfamiliar key in Daddy's underwear drawer. I was there when she found it. I told her that I might know where the key belonged. Together, we went on an investigation to find answers to her suspicion. I thought it unbelievable that Daddy could love some other woman. He had Mommy's love and my love. That had to be more than enough.

Several blocks away, we found it. It was an apartment that Daddy took me by one day, and pointed out that it was a place where he would visit a friend. Mommy and I knocked on the door. No answer. We knocked again. No answer. We used the key, and to our disbelief the door opened.

"Hello? Hello?"

No one answered. We rummaged through drawers and closets looking for something, anything. Then we found them: Daddy's personal belongings... and another woman's. That day was the first of many where we learned that Daddy was living with and loving other women. As the sordid truth became clearer, my days as a carefree, beloved child were over. My days of living in a perpetual breakdown, of sorts, began.

I dealt with my hurt and disbelief in silence, just like Mommy did. Mommy and I didn't talk much about Daddy's other life. I missed and wanted Daddy's time and attention, but I now believed that Daddy did not miss or want mine. I was not good enough for his love; I was not worthy of his time. If my life had no meaning to Daddy, it certainly had no meaning to me.

I went on with my responsibilities as a student, friend, daughter, and sister, while ignoring the pain of my new awareness of Daddy's other life; however, the day came when I just couldn't ignore the pain any longer. In my despair, I decided to take my life. Quietly and secretly, I went to the medicine cabinet where Mommy kept Mercuricome, Vicks Vapor Rub, and aspirin. Mommy always dispensed aspirin to my siblings and me, because she never wanted us to take more than the recommended dosage for our ages. She was asleep when I saw the aspirin, so while unsupervised, I decided to take more than the recommended dosage. As I pulled the aspirin bottle from the shelf, I hesitated, as a voice inside my head cautioned:

"Mommy would be so angry if she knew. You shouldn't do this."

As soon as I considered putting the pills back, a different voice inside my head commanded:

"Quickly, get them; hide them in your pocket."

The first voice countered:

"But mommy would be so upset, so mad."

The second voice impatiently responded:

"Hurry! Get them and put them in your pocket."

And so I obeyed the second voice. On the couch I studied the pills clenched in my hands. "Should I? Shouldn't I? Should I? Shouldn't I?" I popped the pills in my mouth, closed my eyes and swallowed.

I waited to die.

Instead, I fell asleep…

…and awakened to another unhappy day with myself and my life without Daddy.

I was a confused and deeply hurt little girl. I grew to hate my Daddy. I stopped calling him "Daddy" and began referring to him as my father. I didn't understand how my secure life, which was the center of my father's love and attention, could suddenly change, almost overnight. I didn't understand. I didn't understand. I just didn't understand! Confused about this turn of events and angry with him, I carried these feelings into adulthood, and subsequently, motherhood. The confusion, hurt, and anger became embedded deep in my spirit, where they lay dormant, much like the life-cycle of the chicken pox virus, which embeds itself in the cells of the host and remains quiet for years. Through some set of circumstances, usually related to stress, the chicken pox virus awakens and manifests itself as the dreaded shingles.

My pain and anger were never acknowledged and released, but they instead remained dormant for decades. They influenced my relationship with myself and with others, rendered me silent when I should have spoken, made me speak when I should have remained silent, made me drink when I should have remained alert, and made me feel inadequate and insecure when I really was competent.

LESSON APPLICATION

I took an online survey[2] that is designed to assess the quality of a daughter's relationship with her father. With only ten questions to answer, I wasn't convinced the survey could accurately assess my relationship with my father. However, I decided to answer the questions anyway. I was surprised at the results, which I post here:

THE DISAPPOINTED DAUGHTER

Your father might as well be a stranger you met in the street. It's a chilly relationship between the pair of you, and you are quite aware of this. You are distanced from each other and there is no strong tie. You probably need to grieve for the father you can't have and get on with finding the real you. You were, at least, given a certain amount of independence when you were growing up, and you have been able to get on with life despite the father-shaped gap. Yet this has also made you slightly distant with other people, especially men, who you always fear will disappoint you. You feel persistent regret at the fact that you have missed the chance to get to know your father. You started off with a negative image of him (perhaps encouraged by what your mother has said) but ended up blaming yourself, coming to the conclusion that you weren't worth his love. You think to yourself: if my own father's not even interested in me, what do I expect other men to see in me? Inside there is a little girl who doesn't understand where it all went wrong. Your father has failed to do his job and he doesn't know how to show his feelings towards you. Try and talk to him. Better late than never — it's still possible to form a bond. If you have already tried to contact him and have had no response, try to build your self-esteem and remind yourself that not all men are like him. Plenty of them would relish the chance to get to know you… and love you too.

This description was spot-on. It was so accurate, in fact, that I thought it important to understand this dynamic relationship. I was not the only daughter with a hole-in-her-heart pain.

According to associate professor of philosophy at Eastern Kentucky University, Michael Austin, editor of <u>Fatherhood - Philosophy for Everyone: The Dao of Daddy</u>[3],

> "A father's influence in his daughter's life shapes her self-esteem, self-image, confidence and opinions of men. "How Dad approaches life will serve as an example for his daughter to build off of in her own life, even if she chooses a different view of the world."

In her article, "How Dads Shape Daughters' Relationships,"[4] Dr. Jennifer Kromberg writes:

> "If there was a dad or other male caregiver in your early life, he probably set the first model of how a relationship with a man would be. And for better or for worse, regardless of circumstances,

children love their parents/caregivers unconditionally and accept the attachment and love that is (or is not!) given in return as normal. Our first attachment patterns shape our expectations for future attachments. Overtly and also unintentionally, our parents teach us how to approach our lives and relationships – they teach us how to express and receive love, how to handle disagreements, how to process feelings, etc. Our parents shape and color the lens through which we see and organize meaning about other human interactions."

There are many more articles, much research conducted, and books written about the father-daughter relationship. You probably know, intuitively, that this relationship (or the lack of it) is critical for a daughter's healthy emotional and psychological development. But, what do you do when that relationship is hurt, damaged, broken? How do you begin to heal? There is hope and you can heal. Two important points for healing are offered by essayist and award-winning journalist, Melissa T. Shultz. In her article in the Huffington Post,[5] she offers these two points and a concluding thought:

1. It's not your fault. You were just a kid. All kids deserve to be loved and protected. Don't blame yourself for what your father did or didn't do.

2. Write about it, talk about it -- turn it into art. By sharing our wounds we open up our hearts and healing happens. I know. I've seen it firsthand.

The bottom line is this: A negative relationship with your father will only come to define you if you let it. Don't let the past determine your present, and your future. As mature adults, we have the power to set the course of our lives. Remember that -- we have the power. Let's use it.

Yes, let's set our own course for our lives. Let's begin with admission of any brokenness, big or small. Admission is a place where healing can begin.

YOUR TURN

What was the turning point in your life and how did you get through it? Did your father have any part in your turning point?

_____

_____

_____

_____

_____

_____

_____

_____

_____

_____

_____

_____

_____

_____

_____

_____

"But he said to me, 'My grace is sufficient for you, for my power is made perfect in weakness.' Therefore I will boast all the more gladly about my weaknesses, so that Christ's power may rest on me."

- 2nd Corinthians 12:9, New International Version

LESSON

2

"I Can't Take It Anymore!" Does Not Mean You're Ready To Surrender.

It was the 2,190th day. This was the total number of days I had been fulfilling my responsibility as a full-time mother. The morning was bustling with the usual busyness of getting my three young children off to school. I was holding it all in too. Inside, a tidal wave was forming. I knew it. I could feel it. After driving my three children to school and escorting them all to their respective classrooms, I wobbled my six-months-pregnant body back to the car and drove home. On the short ride back home, the tidal wave hit shore, and it hit hard. I broke down in tears. Banging hard on my steering wheel, I wasn't exactly crying; I was wailing! I was in emotional pain. The only thing that I could scream repeatedly to God was: "I-Can't-Take-It-Anymore!!!!!!!!!!!!!!!!!!!!!!!!!!!!" While tears were streaming down my face, snot was trickling over my lips and into my mouth. I didn't care.

What set me off that morning? The 2,190th day was the same routine as any other: getting three kids up and ready for school; dropping them off to school; going back home and taking care of family affairs and a 3-bedroom house; picking the kids up from school six hours later; and so on. What the hell was wrong with me on day 2,190? After all, didn't my life appear perfect? I had "everything" reasonable: 3½ beautiful kids; a nice home in a great school district and safe community; good friends; food on my table; a car to drive; clothes to wear (more than I would ever need); a spouse who came home every night, paid the bills, and was a good father; good health; and dental insurance.

But my life was NOT "perfect." By outside appearances, it did seem perfect. But on the inside, NO! My life was painful. Day-in and day-out, I was consumed with the tasks of caring for children, a husband, and a home, all of which I secretly found completely unfulfilling.

In my imagination, day 2,190 might have been a very different scenario. That day would have gone something like this:

> Over the hospital intercom, the nurse calls, "Dr. Pamela Elaine, please see patient in room 202. Dr. Pamela Elaine, room 202, please." I rush to room 202 to see my patient, knowing she is about to transition. The sickly, slowly dying 85-year-old woman, still beautiful, looks straight into my eyes. She utters an unexpected request: "Doctor, would you mind singing that song again? You know the song. Can you sing it to me one more time?" Of course I know exactly the song to which she is referring: "The Best is Yet to Come," recorded by Cynthia Clawson on her album, "You Are Welcome Here,"[6] 1981.

> My patient closes her eyes, slowly, with a smile on her face. Today would not be her final moment, as the staff feared. She would live several more days after hearing the melody of her heart's desire. And I had the honor of participating in her extension.

This imagination was far from my current reality and an improbability in either my immediate or distant future. Wiping noses, kissing boo-boos, chauffeuring, cooking, cleaning, grocery shopping, helping with homework, and planning and supervising play dates ensured that this imagination would never be fulfilled.

What became unbearable was not only the reality of being where I currently was in my life, but also being where I hadn't thoughtfully planned to be. More specifically, I could no longer take the responsibility of being a mother (and child number four hadn't even arrived yet), when being a high-powered doctor, who sang while caring for her patients, was what I thought I really wanted.

Admitting the fact that "I can't take it anymore" did not come easily. I have a strong will and think (sometimes falsely) that I can handle anything. Moreover, admitting that I couldn't take being where I was and where I hadn't planned to be was the ultimate acknowledgement of vulnerability. And being vulnerable - as I mistakenly believed - was the same as being weak.

Yet in my weakness, I could not accept God's grace or God's power, which would have allowed me to be honest with myself and others about my daily tasks and how they had little to do with my true desire. I continued to go through the motions of pretending and smiling, while dying inside. I had not yet surrendered my way (which was to continue with my daily routine and keep quiet about my pretense) to God's way. God's way is an authentic life measured by surrender. In a surrendered life, I allow God to take my weakness (i.e., pretense) and use it to transform my life and that of others. In a surrendered life, weakness, then, is no longer weakness, but strength.

Surrender means:

> To AGREE to stop fighting, hiding, resisting, etc., because you know that you will not win or succeed; to give the control or use of (something) to someone else.
>
> - Merriam Webster

What a valiant effort I maintained, pretending to be happy and fulfilled being a mother, sacrificing the desires of my heart until who knows when, putting others' needs before my own because that is what was expected, fighting against my own feelings of depression, and being inauthentic to everyone around me, including myself. Certainly, I WAS NOT WINNING!

I finally admitted that, "I can't take it anymore." However, while admitting this fact was no doubt an important step, it was only a partial step. A surrendered life is one where the woman can state boldly, "I can't take it anymore...and I surrender." I couldn't surrender yet. I had too much control (or so I thought) that I wasn't ready to give up, and I could not bear the consequence of having people learning that I really DIDN'T have it altogether. Eventually, I would have no choice but to surrender... in a pool of tears on my bathroom floor!

LESSON APPLICATION

Every human being practices control in one form or another: over others, ourselves, money, relationships, work, children, spouse, minority groups, food consumption, even the weather. "I can't take it anymore" is the most important landmark on the path to relinquishing control and living a surrendered life. However, as human beings, we are uncomfortable with the lack of control. We live in a society where having control is valued, measured, and considered powerful. Surrender, however, implies weakness. So, naturally, we run quickly from the very thought of surrender.

Before running away, let's take a deeper look into the "black box" of control and surrender.

Being in control and having a need for control are important distinctions. The former is considered to be positive (to be in control) while the latter is considered to be negative (a need for control). A need for control carries a negative connotation. Who wants to hang out with a friend or lover who NEEDS to be in control? Yet, this need is exactly what drives us to control. It is a need, and so by definition, it must be met or one's survival is at stake. If we acknowledge and accept that we need to control, we may more readily surrender. But, we will talk about surrender in a bit. Right now, let's keep looking into the "black box" of our need to control.

Psychologists say our need to control is usually based on three basic things: fear, unworthiness, and a lack of trust:

1. **Fear** – that things won't turn out the way we'd like; or that we'll get hurt; or that bad things will happen; or, or, or.....
2. **Unworthiness** – we don't feel like we deserve help, support, or don't believe that things should go our way
3. **Lack of trust** – we don't count on others and don't believe that things will be okay if we are not managing every aspect of a situation, circumstance, conversation, or relationship

However, the need for control is not a bad thing. In fact, it has a biological basis[7]. Humans need control, and this need is expressed as either **choice** or

power. Imagine how you would feel if you could not choose where to live, what to buy, or whom you could love. What if these choices were not available to you? You wouldn't feel like you were truly alive. You would feel limited, confined. Imagine if you didn't have the power to obtain an education, hire and fire staff, or make business or family decisions? Again, you would feel limited and confined. Experts in the field of psychology suggest, from review of the evidence, that control is part of our biology. That means we can't help but to control. It's in our nature! These experts draw the following conclusions about control[8]:

> "…but what is important…is that the exercise of choice acts to energize and reinforce an individual's sense of agency [or, one's belief in her ability to succeed in specific situations]. Anything that undermines this perception of control may be harmful to an individual's well-being."

> "…the evidence suggests the desire to exercise control, and thus, the desire to make choices, is paramount for survival."

> "Just as we respond to the physiological needs (e.g. hunger) with specific behaviors (i.e. food consumption), we may fill a fundamental psychological need by exercising choice. While eating is undoubtedly necessary for survival, we argue [authors] that exercising control may be critical for an individual to thrive. Thus, we [authors] propose that exercising choice and the need for control – much like eating and hunger – are biologically motivated."

> "The perception of control seems to play an important role in buffering an individual's response to environmental stress."

If control is a biological phenomenon like hunger, there must also exist a "proper" or "beneficial" way to satisfy one's biological nature. For example, if every time you are hungry and set out to consume a Big Mac, large fries and a large Coke[9] for lunch, certainly you have satisfied your hunger (your biological need), right? However, you just consumed 1330 calories[10] (in one meal), 54 grams of fat[11], and 1320mg of sodium[12]. And that was just lunch! Dinner and breakfast haven't even been considered yet. Keep up this type of eating, and you are well on your way to high blood pressure, obesity, and diabetes. A proper or beneficial way to satisfy your hunger might be (keeping with the McDonald's analogy) a Southwest salad (without the dressing) with grilled chicken and large water (with a slice of lemon or lime to splurge). Your dietary consumption, alternatively, is 290 calories, 8g of fat and 650mg of sodium. Big difference!

If control is part of our biology and thus needs to be expressed, there is at least one "beneficial" way to express it (much like the Southwest salad rather than the Big Mac). One beneficial way is through surrender to a Higher Power, or (your) God's power.

The psychologists conclude the following from their findings:

> "In the absence of sufficient knowledge or resources to make an optimal decision, choice by a proxy agent, such as a trusted friend, family member, or physician, may be more desirable than personal choice. In any case, individuals are still exercising control by choosing to engage in or to abstain from decisions to promote their best interest."

I did not think I had control over my personal life as a wife and mother. To satisfy the biological need, however, I attempted to control others (also called "illusion of control"), like my children. I tried to control what they wore, how they behaved, whom they played with, what they ate, what extracurricular activities they participated in, etc. Yet, controlling them wasn't working very well. I felt controlled instead, but kept working hard to maintain the illusion of control right up to the point of emotional exhaustion.

Spiritual teachers tell us that the best way to gain control is to surrender it because surrender is, paradoxically, power. These teachers name many benefits of a surrendered life, including:

- Joy
- Peace
- Freedom
- Energy
- Creativity
- Support
- Ease
- Connection
- Love

In her article, *The Art of Surrender*[13], published in <u>Psychology Today</u>, author Jennifer Hamady wrote:

> "Surrender does not make us powerless; it sets us free…we can choose to cultivate the practice of surrender in the face of any and every circumstance, which always leads to a greater level of aliveness, effectiveness, and joy."

Surrender can be as effortless as making the statement, "I surrender." This is a statement that you have to make daily, if not hourly. But if you are not ready to surrender control, as I wasn't, at least admit, "I can't take it anymore." That's good enough as a first step to a powerful life led by surrender to God, a Higher Power.

YOUR TURN

In what area of your life do you want to scream, "I can't take it anymore?" Are you willing to surrender that area to God or your Higher Power?

_____

_____

_____

_____

_____

_____

_____

_____

"More than anything, I wanted her to know that she was not alone..."

- Phyllis N. Hicks

LESSON

3

"When You Can't Take It Anymore...Surrender."

I couldn't stop crying. The more I told myself to stop, the harder I cried. Downstairs, in the basement of my home, my crying episode erupted unexpectedly and in the worst of company. Panicked, my seven-year-old grabbed the phone and called her father at work: "Mommy is crying and she won't stop." My husband calmly instructed my seven-year-old to wait while he called one of my friends. She would know what to do until he got home, and home he would be shortly.

By the time my husband arrived, I had gone upstairs, taken all of the keys to the bathroom door, and locked myself in the powder room. On the small, cold linoleum floor I continued to sob. My body heaved with each teardrop. By then, the children were out of their minds with confusion and despair. They couldn't understand in their innocence how their mother – the one always in control – was clearly out of control.

My husband finally arrived. My seven-year-old led him to where I was. He knocked on the bathroom door and called out my name to open it. I ignored him. He knocked again. I continued to ignore him. The more he knocked, the more I ignored. Finally, he got the message and stopped knocking. I didn't want to talk to him and have to muster some academic explanation for my behavior that he might find acceptable. In my desperate state, he was the last person I believed could help me. In my mind, he and the four little people standing outside the bathroom door were leeches waiting to suck the blood out of my body...again. It was because of them, I thought, that I was in this wretched state.

Outside the bathroom door, voices fell quiet. The next knock on the door was the soft voice of my friend, Phyllis. Immediately understanding my predicament (because certainly she had been in a pickle like this once or twice herself), she whispered:

"Pam, I love you. It's okay. You can open the door."

Without hesitation, I unlocked the door. She entered quickly and locked the door behind her, fell to the floor, and wrapped her arms around me. She repeated over and over again:

"I love you, Pam. Pam, I love you."

She just rocked me and held me. She asked no questions. She gave no lecture. She offered no reassuring "She's okay, folks!" to the anxious crowd waiting outside the bathroom door.

Somehow, my friend, Phyllis, peeled me off the bathroom floor and took me for a ride. We left without a word to the rest. Fortunately, my husband had appropriately distracted the children, so they didn't even care about my leaving. Phyllis drove me around the city, and she just talked while I listened. She reassured me that I was okay, that what I was feeling was normal, that she had been in the same place many times before. We ended up at a diner, drank coffee, and finally, I began to talk. I tried to explain how deeply despaired I felt and quickly tried to come to some resolution, perhaps a quick fix. But I couldn't, and she didn't expect that of me. When I felt more in control of my emotions and felt I had emptied my soul of the acute pain I was in, Phyllis drove me back home.

But, the pain I was in was not acute. It was chronic. "Acute," by definition, is pain that can be severe, but lasts a relatively short time. Certainly, my pain lasted a few hours on that day, but it soon returned, as it had in the past. "Chronic," on the other hand, is pain that persists or progresses over a long period of time. The emotional, physical, and spiritual pain I felt had been escalating for years. It would often peak in the form of some sort of fit on my part: like screaming at my kids in my over-reaction to something dumb; screaming at my husband in my over-reaction to something even dumber. Then, it would subside. Never had it culminated into an episode of such uncontrollable crying, while holding me hostage in a powder room.

On the cold linoleum floor of that powder room, the realization that my life was not making me happy in a way that I had imagined had finally come full circle. I was living a life I had not imagined for myself, and I did not have the courage to admit that I felt unhappy and certainly unfulfilled. Who would believe that? Who would sympathize? After all, I am a mother, and I am supposed to be superwoman. I am expected to have it all together. So, I kept going, faking it. This is what one does when she does not believe that what she needs to be happy and fulfilled really matters: she gives up what she needs or just keeps quiet about it. Sadly, relinquishing those needs that lead to self-fulfillment is an act of emotional and spiritual suicide -- an unhealthy state for my children, my husband, and me.

That day, I hit "rock bottom." "Hitting rock bottom" is an idiom that means to reach the lowest possible level or to be in the worst possible situation. Most people are familiar with this idiom as it relates to alcoholics or drug abusers (or other addicts). In this situation, addicts either die or reinvent themselves.

I was an "addict" of sorts. I wasn't addicted to drugs or substances. I was addicted to putting everyone's needs first, while neglecting my own. Day after day, year after year, this was my ritual. The "high" from the stress of being wife and mother to four children was deleterious. I couldn't see the toxic build-up of constant stress in my blood stream. Without the relief that self-care would have provided, hitting rock bottom was inevitable, and I didn't even know it. My daily tasks of giving baths, washing clothes, grocery and Costco-shopping, cooking meals, making, bagging, and packing lunches into backpacks, cleaning the kitchen, driving children to and from school, putting other children on the school bus, driving children to play dates and staying for them, checking and supervising homework, refereeing arguments, changing diapers, picking out school clothes, kissing boo-boos over and over again (when the pain lasted beyond 20 seconds), reading bedtime stories, and tucking all into bed one by one meant there was no time for ME. I did these tasks seamlessly, while I kept my hair groomed, my clothes clean, my body washed, my teeth brushed, and said "yes" to sex, whether I wanted to or not.

For several years, while I worked full-time, I would get up daily and arrive to work on time. Friends would marvel and ask, "How do you do it?" I never had a good answer, because I really didn't know. Perhaps I was doing what was necessary, just like a "functional" alcoholic does. However, while I seemed to be functioning well by all outward appearances, I really wasn't. I started eating more and gaining weight (reaching 30 pounds in excess); my blood pressure was in the "hypertensive" range; I was depressed; and I felt spiritually disconnected and didn't attend church regularly.

My children saw me hit rock bottom, and I witnessed how emotionally affected they were. For that, I am grateful. Hitting rock bottom was my wake-up call that said gently and in no uncertain term, "If you don't make your well-being a priority, your husband will suffer, your children will suffer, and you will become extinct."

Instead of becoming extinct, I decided to live and figure out how to make living a joy. With the support of many amazing friends, my family, my children, and the father of my children, I figured out what I had to do and WHO I had to become. In the rest of this book, I share this learning with you so that you might find your own joy and live to the fullest!

LESSON APPLICATION

This Lesson Application is different from the previous and future ones in this book. Instead of offering a lesson to you, I offer the perspective of my dear friend, Phyllis, who rescued me from the bathroom floor that unforgettable day. Below, she shares what she remembers, and offers her thoughts and reflections.

I am a friend of Pamela Elaine. I chose those first four words deliberately. They remind me that I, too, struggle with my identity; that I, too, have wrestled with destiny. And I, too, have collapsed in pain and despair on the hard tile of disappointment.

When I answered the phone that afternoon, I recognized the voice, but it was the words that captured my attention. "Pam has locked herself in the bathroom. I need you to come over."

I don't remember my exact words, but I think they were simply, "I'm on my way." And I was. I told my family I had to go, and since I often received urgent calls in my professional life, there was no extensive questioning.

I drove the short distance to my friend's house and went straight to the first floor bathroom. "It's me, Pam. Open the door." She did. I entered and locked the door again. I did not ask questions, I simply held her, rocked slightly back and forth, and told her I loved her. I knew the bottom of that cavern. I had been there.

I also knew that we were not made for pain, and eventually, our hearts will look up, searching for a sliver of light.

I waited. "Pam I love you." Love: the only gift I could offer; the only gift that can survive the throes of pain and confusion and desperation.

"Do you want to go somewhere and talk?" I think I said. She nodded.

I stood, took her hand, and unlocked the door.

"We are going out." I announced to the anxious faces outside the door. And we left.

I drove. The silence continued. I chose a diner a few small towns over, one that would stay open no matter how long we needed to stay. I don't remember much of our conversation. I listened and I shared. More than anything I wanted her to know that she was not alone, although I had no answers, no solutions, and no remedies. Like lepers in the days of our Lord, I had the same disease, causing me to live outside the city of certainty and joy. And like the leper in Luke 5:12, I knew that only He could heal the soreness in our souls. When she was ready, I drove Pam home.

I prayed for her, as I had often prayed for myself…

for wholeness versus rightness,

for joy versus pain,

for love versus fear.

- Phyllis

YOUR TURN

Have you ever had a breakdown? If so, what did you learn from it? If not, did you ever help a friend get through her breakdown?

_____

_____

_____

_____

_____

_____

_____

_____

_____

_____

_____

_____

_____

_____

_____

_____

_____

_____

The
Breakup

> *"When in despair, look to the oyster's pearl, which holds the secret to transform an irritant into a beautiful gift."*
>
> *- Pamela Elaine*

LESSON

4

You Will Go Through the Dark Tunnel Of Divorce...Why Not In Red, Sexy High Heels?

You may think the tunnel long and narrow
Graffiti'd by the blood of moms in peril
Indeed the tunnel is long, that's just a fact
Don't worry, moms already through it got your back
We are warriors, courageous and strong
'Though in our darkness, didn't know where we belonged.

You must remember - going thru the deep
That pain of Irritation does not equal defeat
Lonely, for sure, the tunnel will feel
Go through it anyway 'cuz what will reveal
Is a sacred beauty all will admire
Illuminated through you if you aspire...

...Aspire to transform pain into a pearl
Suitable to adorn you and the world.
Go ahead and show-off what has become
You, The Pearl! You are the one
Who courageously walked the long path out
Through darkness and danger to triumph without a doubt.

Break-ups happen, this is not new
May I offer something for you to do?
Be gracious as you heal from the pain you are in
After all, this is how the oyster's pearl begins
Honor your strength, resilience and pride
Because it is when your happiness comes alive.

- *Pamela Elaine*

This is a lesson that was very hard to write. Many days, I sat at my laptop and stared at the blank page. I wrote one paragraph, and then deleted it, only to write another paragraph and delete it too. I couldn't get my thoughts together, and I had a hard time just sitting my buns down to write. I didn't know what I wanted to say about my breakup. None of my sentences held together, and I wrote a lot of babble. Writing about divorce was a topic I really wanted to avoid. I had to have a few glasses of wine just to write one page. What made writing about this topic so difficult that I needed a glass of red medicine each time I attempted? I couldn't figure it out.

During a weekly consultation with my Productivity Coach, Mindy (if you don't have one, get one!), I shared with her my roadblock in completing this last chapter. "I'm just not being productive...at all," I bemoaned. "In fact, I avoid writing when I know I need to." Mindy asked a simple question: "Why is this chapter on divorce so much more difficult than the other chapters?" I paused to ponder her question, having never given much thought to it in the past. Her question was a valid one because writing about my breakdown on my bathroom floor in front of my children certainly should have been a difficult chapter to write, but it was actually one of the easiest. Patiently, she waited for me to do an internal investigation (as a skilled Professional Coach should do). The answer came to me: "Because I feel guilty. I feel guilty that I am so happy now as a divorced mother, when I believe I should be unhappy and regretful, like many divorced women are expected to feel. After all, what woman in her right mind would divorce and walk away from a good man and sexual partner who is well-educated, successful, and affords her the opportunity to attend social events with other influential couples, a five bedroom house with a pool in the affluent suburbs of Philadelphia, the privilege of interacting daily with her children and greeting them when they arrive home from a school located in a top-notch school district, and health and dental insurance. I traded all that in exchange for: singlehood, abstinence, a two-bedroom apartment with four kids, partial custody of our children, city life, dateless social outings, loss of health and dental insurance, and living alone without a full-time job. Is this crazy or what? From the outside looking in, it would appear that I lost my mind.

But I didn't lose my mind. I made the decision to divorce with eyes wide open, a clear conscience, good legal counsel, and the driving force behind the scene: a hunger to know me --the person, and in that knowing, to become a greater version of myself. More than 18 years ago, I lost myself in the noble role of wife and mother. I was an empty, unhappy shell, carrying out the functions of my roles and responsibilities, while simultaneously dying inside.

I also felt guilty for another reason: hurting many people and putting them in a position to have to choose between my former spouse and me. I hurt for my former spouse, my children, my parents, my in-laws, and many friends, some of whom, sadly, are no longer friends.

Although I made the decision to divorce with clarity and purpose, the pain was no less gut-wrenching. I cried, even wailed many, many days and nights. I would not wish divorce on my worst enemy. Divorce was like going through a dark tunnel that was lonely, smelly, and full of traps set by Creepy Creatures and Vermin (Irritants). These Creepy Creatures and Vermin at times lunged unexpectedly from tunnel crevices or rose from the muddy ground to latch on to my face, neck, back, arms, and legs. Their howling sounds were deafening, and their presence blocked the distant light that I so desperately needed to keep in view, for hope's sake. At times, my progress through the dark tunnel was reset when these Irritants formed a coup, leaving me emotionally and physically weakened, drained, and bloodied.

How could I ever emerge from this mess when I was severely hampered by unrelenting Irritants that sought to destroy my healing, happiness, and progress? How would I ever come to know myself in order to become a better version of me? Not easily, but possibly by way of courage--courage to transform a painful experience into a purposeful one.

At first, I wrestled with these Irritants that manifested in the forms of arguments with my former spouse, contentious text messages back and forth, name-calling (mostly me), disagreements over custody, accusations of wrong-doing, insults, and mean-spirited behavior. Courage was a choice. It was incumbent upon me to make the choice to stop blaming my former spouse for being the initiator of these Irritants, and to instead thoroughly examine me to see if I was the cause of their constant manifestation. Whether or not my former spouse deserves the blame for initiating some of these Irritants is not the point, nor is it productive to dwell upon. The point is that I had inner work to do, and I made the choice to accept that challenge.

Finding the courage to choose the difficult task of introspection was the first step. I didn't arrive at the doorstep of courage on my own. My closest friends and my family inspired courage within me because they believed in me and believed that I could and would get through the tunnel. Furthermore, they patiently and unwaveringly listened to and supported me in whatever I needed to get through the darkness.

The second step was to move from choice to action. The most significant and profound action I took was enrolling in the Curriculum for Living offered by Landmark, two months after my divorce. The Curriculum for Living is comprised of the following courses: 1) The Landmark Forum; 2) The Advanced Course; 3) Seminar Series; and 4) The Self Expression and Leadership Program. From August of 2013 until April of 2014, I immersed myself in the learning of each course, studying and applying the breakthrough technology for which Landmark Worldwide is well known. This was not easy! Let me say that again, "This was NOT easy!" My ideas of blaming and making others pay for my pain was consistently challenged until I finally had to relinquish this way of thinking to a superior way of being. Landmark's model is ontological, which they explain basically means their programs involve inquiring into the nature and function of being for human beings. The model - rather than providing theories or hypotheticals - provides direct access to what shapes and limits people's day to day lives, and opens up new possibilities for effectiveness and quality of one's life. As human beings, we have choices that make almost anything **possible** in our lives, including getting through dark tunnels where Irritants prey!

The final course in the Curriculum for Living is the Self Expression and Leadership Program. In this course, the participants are guided in the creation of a project that expresses not only who they are fundamentally, their "voice," but who they are that adds value to the greater community. I chose to create a video story of mothers who bounced back from divorce--strong, determined, and beautiful. I called my project "Resilient Beauties," and posted the video on YouTube and other social media sites. The project was healing for me as well as encouragement for mothers going through the dark tunnel of divorce. This project helped to clarify my passion--that which I am willing to live for and even die for: "to help mothers get through the pain of divorce so they can move on to a beautiful life." I have always been attracted to helping others heal through difficulty; that's why I wanted to become a doctor. I continue to create videos of resilience from the amazing stories of mothers who made it through the tunnel. This work is satisfying beyond description.

Divorce and beauty are traditionally never seen as a likely pair. However, to me, they are passionate lovers. Being divorced was a surprising and unexpected gift. It opened up an opportunity for me to define who I wanted to be and pursue her like a lover pursues a soul mate. Yet, I don't know how I could have gotten through the dark tunnel without the support of my family, closest friends, and the instructors of The Curriculum for Living. Much like the story of the Alchemist[14] by Paulo Coehlo, collectively, they "conspired" to enable me to transform the Irritants of divorce into a Pearl. And that pearl...? Well, she's me!

LESSON APPLICATION

The oyster offers a lesson. The oyster is an interesting creature. It is not attractive. In fact, it's kind of...well...ugly, in my opinion. The oyster's outer shell is rough and dull. Physically, it does not command attention. However, open up an oyster and observe its inner surface. It is smooth and vibrant. On the inner shell, you will see a configuration of light and color.

Nestled inside the soft body of specialized oysters can be found a strong and curious crystalline structure that is the substance of a unique gem; a gem that man has sought relentlessly to reproduce. This gem is the pearl. Certain (or specialized) oysters produce pearls within their inner body. The way a pearl is formed naturally by an oyster is an interesting story, which I think relatable to the experience of emerging from the dark tunnel of divorce into a beautiful life.

A natural pearl - one that is untainted by human manipulation - is created quite accidentally by an oyster. Though natural, it is rare for an oyster to produce a pearl. Approximately 1 out of every 15,000 oysters produces a pearl (the reason man gets impatient, bypasses the natural process and makes oysters produce pearls on demand). An oyster lives an uncomplicated, simple, and I believe happy life. In the sea or fresh water, it minds its own business, is stress-free, and feeds on microscopic organisms drifting about (called plankton). Occasionally, while the oyster passively feeds, a grain of sand or parasite (aka, irritant) will lodge itself inside the soft inner body of the oyster, causing the oyster great discomfort. If the oyster is unable to expel the intruder (irritant), the oyster engages in a defense mechanism to protect itself. In this natural defense mechanism, the oyster begins to secrete a smooth, hard crystalline substance around the intruder in order to protect itself. It's much like the defense of the immune response in our bodies when we are sick. This smooth, hard crystalline substance is calcium carbonate-based and is commonly referred to as nacre (pronounced "nay-ker"). As long as the intruder remains within the oyster's body, the oyster will continue to deposit layer upon layer of nacre around it. Each layer makes the encapsulated irritant (the formation of the pearl) more durable, precious, and beautiful. After a few years, the irritant will be totally encased in a smooth and lustrous cocoon of nacre.

Two points of interest: 1) The oyster attempts to dispel the irritant, and when unsuccessful, accepts the irritant as a long-term resident and "befriends" it by encasing it within itself; 2) The oyster's encasing or nacre comes from within its own body. In other words, the oyster's secret defense comes from what is already within the oyster (crystalline substance) rather than something that comes from without. As a result, a pearl is formed. A pearl, then, is a smooth, lustrous, and precious cocoon that contains an intruder or invader, AKA irritant. This production of nature is indeed amazing. The oyster does not intentionally create an object of man's desire because of this irritation. Its only objective is to protect itself so that it can resume the peaceful and happy life it once lived. In other words, from an unfavorable condition, the oyster creates something strong and durable that man has come to recognize and desire.

In fact, the pearl is a prized secret. Humans, with all our technology and science, are still unable to re-create this phenomenon outside of an oyster. Nacre is a soothing substance. It is also composed of millions of microscopic crystals. These crystals are each aligned perfectly so that light passing along the axis of one is reflected and refracted by the other. Light and color are produced in an alluring tapestry.

Most irritants are so small that they can't be seen with the naked eye. They are best viewed under a microscope. Comparatively, the size of a pearl-bearing oyster is between 3 to 9 inches! It is amazing that something so small (invisible to the naked eye) can cause such irritation that an oyster is unable to expel it and is forced to come up with an alternative defense: to create a gem. And gems cannot be compared to one another, as each is unique!

Similarly, a woman who experiences the irritant of divorce is also capable of producing a pearl. However, a pearl cannot be produced in the "fast-food" lane of life. It takes time. In fact, it takes years before the oyster's pearl is produced. It may take time, even years, before a woman's life, after the pain of divorce, produces a pearl. She must cultivate what already exists within her - the beauty that has always been there.

Just as the oyster's cultivation of the pearl becomes the object of man's desire, so will the woman's inner strength become the object the world covets.

So woman, be strong and mighty, understanding that you possess the power to transform what is undesirable into that which is most greatly desired by others. Pain invites you to choose between producing a pearl or living in peril. The choice, Beloved, is yours.

YOUR TURN

What meaning does the story of the oyster hold for you?

_____

_____

_____

_____

_____

_____

_____

_____

_____

_____

_____

_____

"Mothers need to be as passionate about their financial future as they are about their children."

- Pamela Elaine

LESSON

5

Never, Ever Relinquish Your Economic Power.

Finances and budgeting are two aspects of money that I just couldn't stand to talk about. I'd rather get my teeth pulled, and I loathe going to the dentist. Not surprisingly, money, finances, and budgeting were a major conflict in my marriage, as it is in more than 50% of all marriages. Whenever my former spouse reviewed the household budget, I braced myself for an argument. The argument usually began with him announcing, "We need to sit down with the numbers." I would reluctantly join him in the "sit-down," anticipating the outcome. Most of the expenses he would review were the ones incurred by me, and I would get defensive. Then an argument would begin. After a heated discussion and an unproductive "sit-down" session, I would go my way and he would go his.

One night, while he was again examining the household budget, I nervously began to think, "Here we go again." Instead of suggesting that we sit down and discuss the numbers, he declared that he would discontinue what I held as a precious and valuable service: Comcast Cable. He was making an effort to save money each month. I panicked because I wasn't sure if discontinuing Comcast Cable also meant disconnecting high speed Internet--I needed high speed Internet for my children's and for my use. I asked in a defensive tone,

"Does that mean you will be getting rid of high-speed internet service too?"

Unable to elicit an affirmative answer from him, I asked again,

"Does this mean you will be getting rid of high-speed internet service TOO?"

I finally got my answer: "Yes." Guess what I began to do? You guessed it… argue! Well, okay, I actually begged that he at least keep high-speed internet. Searching for the right words that might appeal to his sensibilities, I found myself justifying why it was important to keep the service. In the process, I felt two clear, strong emotions: humiliation and shame--humiliation for begging and shame for not having my own income to pay for it myself. In that moment of begging, I felt completely disempowered, and it was over something seemingly silly, not anything life-altering. Though it wasn't life-changing, it was, however, an awakening to an inconvenient truth.

Later that evening, I admitted this inconvenient truth to myself: I had relinquished my economic power to another, and in doing so, had become vulnerable and submissive to another's decisions. Furthermore, in submitting, I had lost my voice, my power to decide. Yet, I had done so unknowingly. With my support and compliance, he accepted significant employment opportunities that advanced our family's economic well-being. For this I am grateful. Consequently, I sacrificed my own employment and economic opportunities. Resigning from good positions twice during my career enabled him to earn enough to take full responsibility for our finances, while I ensured that he didn't have to worry about the care, safety, and development of our four children. My job, as I saw it, was to hold down the fort at home, so he could bring home the proverbial bacon that I would fry in a pan. I did not fathom the possibility that my support and compliance would result in my loss of economic power. In all fairness to him, he did not ask nor expect me to relinquish my economic power. In fact, he wanted me to be economically "independent." *Unknowingly*, relinquishing my economic power was the consequence of my decision to resign.

Unknowingly is the operative word. I was ignorant of the consequences of depending on someone else to take care of my economic needs and my future. My mother repeatedly admonished my sister and me as we were growing up: "Always have your own money. Never depend on a man." Imbedded in her admonition was not only fear, but wisdom too. I didn't heed her wisdom because I didn't think it was that important, nor did I think I would ever need my own money. Love and commitment in a partnership was all I needed and believed to be important. However, that night as I begged my former spouse to refrain from disconnecting our high-speed internet service as part of his plan to slash the budget, I learned that financially depending on someone else equates to surrendering your own economic power. You in essence lose your decision-making voice, and when this occurs, you risk losing not only the respect of the person you are financially dependent upon, but also your own self-respect. By economic power, I mean the practice of actively earning an income to provide for yourself *and* to decide for yourself what your future will be. Economic power engenders respect, and respect is an absolute necessity in any healthy relationship.

While I made immediate attempts to change my personal economic status, those attempts were futile and inconsistent. What I needed to do was change my attitude about and relationship with money, rather than with my former spouse. After years of giving up my voice, I had distanced myself from money. It became an unfamiliar commodity. I needed to become familiar with it again. My first step was to begin studying the subject of finances. I collected books, listened to audiotapes, and spent time on YouTube investigating money matters. I even joined two money groups on FaceBook! Finally, I took the most important step: connected with a financial advisor who helped me put a financial plan in place for my current state and for my immediate future. The financial advisor put the missing pieces together, and to this day, he is the only man who knows the secrets to my...wealth ☺.

LESSON APPLICATION

Marriage and money have a contentious relationship. Dr. Leon F. Seltzer nails the description of this relationship in his article, "Couples – Stop Fighting Over Money"[15] found in Psychology Today:

> "No question about it. Fighting about money is hazardous to your relationship. One recent study (by Jeffrey Dew at Utah State University) found that the more frequently couples argued over finances, the more likely they were to get divorced—especially if their altercations occurred several times a week, or almost every day. Obviously, couples fight about many things—from child rearing, to sex, to household chores, to dealing with in-laws. But, above everything else, frequency of money disputes remains the single best predictor of divorce.

It's also an area of contention where attitudes of prideful self-righteousness are most likely to prevail. When couples argue about money, their respective positions so deeply reflect core values that it's hard for them not to get into antagonistic gridlock on the subject. And like a festering disease, as time passes such polarization tends not to get better but worse—ultimately threatening the very foundation of their relationship. The inability to appreciate and sympathetically discuss their conflicting attitudes toward money eventuates in all kinds of misunderstandings and hurt feelings, which in turn leads to an increasing sense of alienation and loss of intimacy."

A disturbing statistic reveals that women are twice as likely as men to experience poverty in their later years[16]. As such, there is no reason or justification for a woman to count on anyone else to support her throughout life. This is particularly important in an era of vanishing pensions, questions about the future of Social Security, a volatile labor market, and a high divorce rate.

There are an estimated 85.4 million mothers of all ages in the United States who control approximately $2.1 trillion dollars of spending per year or 85% of household income. Of the 85.4 million mothers, an estimated five million are stay-at-home moms as of 2012. According to Salary.com, if you are a stay-at-home mom, you average 94 hours of work per week, which means you are eligible for $113,000 yearly income on average, or more.

Moms are the ultimate multi-taskers. If we work (which does not necessarily mean that we are financially independent of our spouses), we must juggle not only our own career income and workload, but we must in turn also complete, on average, an additional 58 hours a week fulfilling our household and maternal responsibilities. This extra load makes us eligible for additional earnings of $67,000, yearly.[17] On average, we work over 54 hours of overtime every week. Our hourly wage varies anywhere from $9.95 to $54 per hour. Consider the hourly wage for some of our most common roles:

- Housekeeper – $10.10
- Psychologist – $38.03
- Cook – $13.56
- Day Care Teacher – $13.08
- Computer Operator – $15.82
- Facilities Manager – $31.59
- Driver – $13.61
- CEO – $54.58
- Laundry Operator – $9.95

We are a strong force, collectively. But why is it that so many of us women are financially unaware and leave the business of money to someone else?

Experts offer the following reasons:
- We fear not being able to understand the language of finances.
- We have a misperception that money is complex and that men are better equipped at it than women.
- We believe that finances and investing are traditionally a male-dominated field.
- We lack confidence in investing.
- We do not deal realistically with our future.
- Money is power, and many of us women already lack self-confidence in our personal power.

You don't have to relinquish your economic power to anyone, whether you choose to stay at home and raise a family or go off to work and still raise a family. Whatever your disposition, maintain and build upon your economic self-sufficiency through financial literacy and knowledge. Mothers need to be as passionate about money, finances, and their financial future as they are about their children.

Below are a few steps and resources experts offer that can help you move toward becoming financially literate and independent.

1. Get a financial advisor. Test-drive a few of them until you find one with whom you feel comfortable and can trust. The best way to ensure finding the RIGHT financial advisor is to read, "Tough Questions to Ask Your Advisor." I downloaded these questions for FREE from the National Association of Personal Financial Advisors' website (www.napfa.org and type in "Tough Questions To Ask Your Advisor"). Though this is an easy and practical step, the remaining steps are more emotional, because unlike men, women have an emotional connection to money.

2. Study your past to understand your financial habits and practices. Your money personality affects your money behavior.

3. Talk to your spouse or significant other about your financial up-bringing and how it shaped your relationship with money. If you don't have a partner, talk to a friend or relative. Talking about your relationship with money demystifies money and brings a level of comfort.

4. Start a journal to write down your fears (or concerns) about money (for example, you may be unsure whether you will have enough in which to retire), and write at least one practical way you can face that fear.

5. In your journal, write down your level of faith regarding money (for example, what you would like to accomplish with it).

6. Identify a goal, such as saving $50 per month towards a personal savings account that you will use at your discretion.

Some of my favorite resources that women can use to increase their financial literacy include:

Websites:
- www.dailyworth.com
- www.WIFE.org
- www.wiserwomen.org
- www.fwa.org
- www.kiplinger.com
- www.credit.com

Books, CDs, DVDs:
- Secrets of Six Figure Women, by Barbara Stanny
- Women Who Finish Rich, by David Bach
- The Automatic Millionaire, by David Bach
- How to Be a Couple and Still Be Free, by Tina B. Tessina

Finding a Financial Advisor:

You can always ask friends and relatives for referrals. I also recommend that you visit www.napfa.org (National Association of Personal Financial Advisors), to learn more about financial advisors.

Financial independence for mothers is imperative. In her book, How to Be a Couple and Still Be Free[18], Dr. Tina B. Tessina states: "A woman who has some financial independence is free to state her mind, disagree, ask for what she wants, and a woman who doesn't is not."

According to the National Marriage Project[19], a woman's standard of living can decrease by up to 27 percent after a divorce, while a man's may rise by 10 percent. During my marriage, I ignorantly chose to be financially dependent. Now as a single mother, I am choosing to be financially independent and have a plan by which to do so. Do you?

YOUR TURN

In what ways have you enabled someone else to be responsible for your financial sufficiency (spouse, government, employer)? Does your dependency on this person/entity make you feel empowered or imprisoned? What steps can you take to change your circumstance from dependency to independency?

_____

_____

_____

_____

_____

_____

_____

_____

_____

_____

_____

_____

"The oak fought the wind and was broken, the willow bent when it must and survived."

- Robert Jordan, The Fires of Heaven

LESSON

6

Beauty Is Power!

Donna was bubbling with excitement over the phone. It was Thursday evening, and I was on my way out the door to meet a friend for an engagement. Donna's enthusiasm raised my curiosity. "Pam! Pam!" she shouted. "Stop whatever you are doing right now and check out Dr. Oz's website. Dr. Oz is looking for stories. Sounds just like the conference you are planning."

Dr. Oz? Ha! Might my upcoming conference plans somehow align with THE DR. OZ SHOW? Honestly, I didn't think so—at first.

She explained further: "Dr. Oz is looking for stories about healthy revenge after divorce!"

HUH? HOLD ON! STOP THE PRESS! I appreciated my friend's excitement, but I didn't like what I was hearing: "REVENGE" and "divorce" being used in the same line? Nope! Not for me. I wasn't seeking revenge, nor did I want the world to know I was going through a divorce.

"I don't think so, Donna. I don't feel good about the topic. I'm not trying to get revenge here."

Donna insisted: "I think you should check it out, Pam. It sounds exactly like what you are doing with your upcoming conference."

Donna was helping me plan a conference for women going through divorce. I titled my conference, "You Are Not Alone: Resilience and Reclaiming our Beauty." I planned this conference as an outlet for my personal pain, as I too was going through a divorce. I also wanted to build a community of women who understood that resilience from the pain and disappointment of divorce is possible. I planned to have guest speakers and personal stories to help shed light on how resilience can be achieved through inner beauty. Inner beauty can enable women to emerge powerfully from the devastation of divorce. My conference was designed to inspire the belief that we are not victims. We are victorious!

Donna convinced me to go online and write my story anyway. I trusted Donna, so I did just that. That evening, while riding in the back seat of my friend's car on our way to an engagement, I used my iPhone to type my story onto Dr. Oz's website. Carelessly, I looked over what I wrote, attached a recent photo, then hit the submit button.

I thought to myself, "Done! At least I did what I told Donna I would do. Whatever..."

Though I was careful to double check, I didn't care too much about typos since I wasn't excited about the possibility of appearing on The Dr. Oz Show to discuss this particular topic. Appearing on the show would certainly mean airing my dirty laundry on national television. I figured it was a long shot anyway.

Early Friday afternoon, while I was engrossed in writing a blog about my upcoming conference, my cell phone rang with a number from a (212) area code, which I did not recognize. I rarely answer calls from unknown numbers because they are usually from telemarketers asking me to purchase Viagra, at a discount! I stared at the number while the phone rang twice and then a third time. I finally answered it.

"This is Pamela Elaine." I answered in my most professional voice.

"Hello Pamela. This is Amanda from The Dr. Oz Show."

My ears perked up as she continued.

"We received your submission. I just want to ask you a few questions. Is that okay?"

("Like, yeah," I thought.)

"Suuuuure," I responded calmly.

"Ummm…how long ago was this photo taken that you submitted?"

"About 4 months ago," I replied.

"Great!" She continued, carefully framing her questions and explaining her reason for calling me about the show. I answered each question to the best of my ability. Then I paused and made a bold (aka, dumb) confession:

"Amanda, I am very uncomfortable with the title of this show. I am not seeking revenge in my divorce. That's not my goal at all."

Amanda was reassuring. She explained that Dr. Oz wanted to make a contrast between "unhealthy" ways to get "revenge" from divorce (hence plastic surgery which was the main theme of the show), and "healthy" ways to get revenge (i.e., starting a business, a blog, getting a new look). She said a healthy way of "revenge" isn't revenge at all. It is a statement of a woman's power. "Ohhh!!!" I exclaimed, in a moment of relief.

Amanda went on to explain that my story fit the healthy profile of revenge by starting (resuming in my case) a business. I, along with two other women, would share our individual healthy decisions, which actually didn't involve plastic surgery of any type.

Amanda, sticking to protocol, thanked me for my information and said that IF I were chosen as one of the guests on The Dr. Oz Show, someone else would contact me later that day. Right! I knew I wouldn't be chosen. After all, who raises questions about Dr. Oz's topics and actually gets a call back?

No less than two hours later, I received another call from the same (212) area code. On the other end was a producer from The Dr. Oz Show. He introduced himself and reviewed Amanda's intake questions and my answers. Then he said:

"We would like to have you on the show. Can you be in New York City, 8a.m. on Monday morning?"

(Like, 3-days-from-today-Monday-morning???)

I contained my excitement, and with another bold (aka, dumb) response, I asked:

"Would you mind holding on for a moment while I check my calendar?"

Graciously, he did. While I was checking, I thought to myself: I must be a fool! Who checks her calendar to see if she is available to be on The Dr. Oz Show? Uh…Hello???

"Thank you for holding. Yes, I can be in New York City on Monday morning." The producer went on to give me the specifics. In three short days, I would be in New York to be a guest on The Dr. Oz Show! Amanda followed up with me, sending me information to prepare for the show.

I called Donna and screamed my head off!! I couldn't believe it. Together, we danced for joy over the phone. I called my best friend and she danced for joy with me too. I did not tell my immediate family. I couldn't risk the possibility of negative, cautious, or "Are you sure…" responses.

On Monday morning, I hopped on Amtrak. My commute seemed surreal. Surprisingly, I felt calm. For an hour and fifty minutes I visualized walking up to Dr. Oz, shaking his hand, telling him stories, and sipping coffee together while we talked about healthy revenge.

My train finally arrived, and I proceeded to New York's Rockefeller Center. As instructed, I headed to the NBC studio, checked in, and went through tight security. Upon arrival, I was greeted by Amanda and escorted to the Green Room, where I was offered comfort, tea, and snacks (pinch me somebody).

While in the Green Room, I met the other two women with whom I would share a brief moment in the spot-light. Amanda reviewed my script, which I then edited (I couldn't help myself) and rehearsed, unsuccessfully, over and over again. I couldn't calm my nerves. I couldn't stop thinking about the awful comments some family and friends might make about my admission on national TV. I couldn't stop thinking about the disappointment my spouse might feel, being such a private person. The possibility that he might disapprove of my sharing my story was so discouraging that I kept the opportunity a secret (sort of like what we women do when we buy a pair of ridiculously expensive shoes, "neglect" to tell our husbands, and then hide the shoes long enough for him to not recognize their newness when we finally do wear them).

After Amanda made sure my outfit fit protocol, she escorted me and the two other women to make-up and hair. This was just like TV! One artist refreshed my make-up and another artist styled my hair. Then, I was all set. Amanda escorted me to my "reserved" seat in the studio.

There, sitting in the front section of the studio, with bright lights and a clear view of the stage, I felt honored and humbled and excited. A sacred peace covered my body…until I heard…

"5, 4, 3, 2, 1 and we are LIVE!"

After two amazing women spoke about their healthy revenge, Dr. Oz[20] turned to me and asked:

"So, Pamela, what's your healthy revenge goal and how is that making you a happier person?"

And I shared my story with confidence, like a pro:

"Well, my goal was to have a successful business…so now my company is growing because I decided to coach other mothers to find resilience in their physical, emotional, spiritual and financial beauty, because beauty is power! And so, revenge started out as something negative, but I think I've turned it into something beautiful."

That was it. Three days of preparation ended in 26 seconds of fame. I was escorted back to the Green Room, packed my bags, thanked everyone, and boarded the train for home. I wasn't even disappointed that Dr. Oz and I didn't have a chance to sip coffee and chat a bit.

On the train ride back home, a startling reality became crystal-clear to me – beauty IS power. I actually formed that statement on the spur of the moment. It wasn't at all in the script Amanda gave me. Beauty is power, and resilience IS possible through beauty. Not just physical beauty from plastic surgery, as The Dr. Oz Show attempted to contrast, but beauty that comes from within…inner beauty. I realized that the conference I was planning, "Resilience," and my ability to aid in other women's healing, was an expression of spiritual beauty, a beauty that comes from within. And, every woman has inner beauty. If she taps into that reservoir, she can bounce back from any relationship setback. I have no doubt.

LESSON APPLICATION

Why do some women bounce back from setbacks while others remain stuck? We can contemplate many reasons, such as low self-esteem, anger, resentment, disbelief, and depression. I believe, however, that one fundamental reason explains why: Powerlessness!

Powerlessness is defined as the *belief* or *feeling* that there is nothing you can do to move forward or change your circumstances, feelings, or future. But, you are not powerless. You have the ability to bounce back after a setback because both *beliefs* and *feelings* are within your control to change.

The ability to bounce back is called resilience. Resilience is:

> *The power or ability to return to the original or natural state after being bent, compressed, or stretched.* (Merriam-Webster)

Curious about what our *"original"* state is, I did some research and found interesting information. Your original state is SPIRITUAL. You are a spirit being living in a physical body. The philosopher, Pierre Teilhard de Chardin, said:

> *"We are not human beings having a spiritual experience; we are spiritual beings having a human experience."*

The word "spiritual," as used here, does not mean religious, or the practice of one faith over another. In the most simplistic of definitions I found, "spiritual" means a process of transformation into something greater than oneself. When you experience hurt, disappointment and loss, and feel powerless about it, your spiritual state of existence is *changed* (bent) *from an originally even condition*[21] of joy, peace, love, forgiveness, and faith to:

* Sadness
* Stress
* Hate
* Un-forgiveness
* Doubt

Resilience is a return to a spiritual state of joy, peace, love, forgiveness, and faith when circumstances set you back.

Let's return to the definition of resilience: The power or ability to return to the original or natural state after being bent, compressed or stretched. But where do you get that POWER to bounce back? What's the source of it?

I believe the answer is this: from BEAUTY! Specifically, inner or spiritual beauty is the source of power that enables us to bounce back. Beauty is simply defined as "pleasure" – pleasure experienced in mind, body and spirit. Spiritual Beauty + Resilience = the pleasure of bouncing back...back to a natural state of joy, peace, love, forgiveness, faith.

Ok...wait! Is it really possible to find pleasure in bouncing back to a natural state of spirituality? YES! It is possible through the following practices (and many others):

1. **Forgive others** – Forgiveness is a decision, it is not a feeling. Forgiveness frees you to experience joy, peace, and love. Further, when you release the desire to punish or seek revenge, you attract good into your life and add favor in your circumstances.

2. **Forgive yourself** – What keeps us from forgiving others is the lack of forgiveness of ourselves. The measure of grace you give yourself for your mistakes is the same measure of grace you extend to others in forgiving them.

3. **Meditate (pray or chant)** - Meditation recharges the body and releases stressful feelings and thoughts. Meditation is effective when done consistently, twice a day for at least 20 minutes. You can meditate on a calming sound (in your head or audibly), slow breaths, a sacred thought, gratitude, etc. Meditation is not the same as praying. Praying is speaking while meditation is silence. Meditating quiets your mind so that you can tap into your most creative and generous source.

4. **Accept what is** – We live in a "should be" mindset, holding on to what we think should be and resisting or rejecting what actually is. This mindset can be debilitating and frustrating. Remember the adage, "What you resist, persists." However, when you accept what is, as it is, you lessen its crushing burden and open yourself up to creative problem-solving and new possibilities.

5. **Don't send the nasty text message** – Re-write it. When you get that text message (or email) that makes you want to strangle the sender, write a kind, generous or gracious response instead. You will defuse a potentially volatile exchange, minimize conflict, and feel good at the same time.

6. **Nurture your spirit** – Take time daily, even just 10 minutes, to pursue a hobby or passion. How many days pass by and you don't spend 10 minutes on something that brings you joy, pleasure, or fun?

7. **Spend some quality time with family or friends** – These individuals should make you feel good and you should in turn make them feel good. This is mutually beneficial. You do not have to spend time with family and friends that you aren't crazy about during this sacred time of resilience. You can work on those "challenging" relationships once you feel confident that you are back on track.

8. **Make someone else happy** – By far, this is the most satisfying and greatest healing practice of resilience because it is beneficial no matter what you desire to accomplish. When you practice making someone else happy, happiness is returned to you.

Energy (or effort) is required to bounce back from life's set-backs. Bouncing back is a conscious and intentional decision. Cultivate and practice inner beauty. Inner beauty is the fuel (energy) to bounce back. Practice makes perfect. Remain committed to the practice because one morning you will awaken and realize that inner beauty is no longer a conscious effort, it is who you are. In that realization, you will come to know that you were not made to be broken, but to bend.

YOUR TURN

What is the setback that keeps you feeling broken? Which method above to achieve inner beauty could you implement consistently, and how would that practice make a difference in your circumstances?

_____

_____

_____

_____

_____

_____

_____

_____

_____

_____

_____

_____

_____

_____

_____

_____

_____

_____

The Breakthrough

"The cave you fear to enter holds the treasure you seek."

- Joseph Campbell

LESSON

7

Face Your Fear.

My mother was packing a delicious picnic basket of fried chicken, bologna sandwiches, and Kool-Aid, while my dad was packing the fishing rods and bait. Today was going to be the best day of the week. My mom, dad, sister, brother, and I were heading to the San Pedro pier to fish. I enjoyed going fishing with my family because it was a fun pastime that brought us closer together.

When we arrived at the pier, my senses came alive. I could smell the saltiness of the sea and hear its waves banging playfully against the rocks. I could see the fish anxiously awaiting their meal and feel the cool breeze as it waltzed over the waves. Mom unpacked the picnic basket while dad assembled the fishing rods and placed bait on the hooks. I already knew how to fish. My dad taught me when I was younger. Now that I was a big girl at the age of seven, he didn't need to teach me anything more. I stood on the edge of the pier, looking directly at the fish. I wanted to touch them.

"Don't get too close to the edge of the pier," Mom cautioned. She didn't need to do so because I had stood on the edge of this pier a dozen times. I stepped back from the edge, just so she would feel better. Hungry, I sat down near her for a bite of her delicious fried chicken.

A short time later, I wanted to see the progress my dad, brother, and sister were making with catching fish, so I left my mother's side and went back to the edge of the pier. Fascinated by the fish below, I bent over and tried to reach into the water to touch one. They were too far away, so I reached further and longer. As I bent down, I lost my balance and tumbled right into the sea-- head first. I started sinking. In a complete panic, I tried to keep my head above the surface, but it was a struggle. As I looked up, I could see my sister perched on the edge of the pier reaching out her hand to grab me. I couldn't reach her! I just could not reach her because we were too far apart. I was sinking faster and faster, so it seemed. Suddenly, as quickly as I fell in, I was pulled up and out of the water and back onto the pier. My sister saved me! Mommy quickly dried me off, packed our bags and the picnic basket, and put us in the car. During the ride home, I repeatedly thanked my sister...

– STOP –

You know this story already, right? You read it in Lesson 1 (if you didn't, take a moment to read it now). This story in Lesson 1 is about more than learning my father was my hero/rescuer. This story is about fear, fear of large bodies of water.

When flying in an airplane over the ocean, I'd panic inside. When driving over a bridge, I couldn't help but imagine falling in and drowning, trapped inside my car. I was growing tired of this feeling and rather annoyed by the control it had over me. Yet, there was nothing I could do about this fear, or so I thought. Fear is the monster that never leaves. I was resigned to be afraid of large bodies of water for the rest of my life. Fear became the ruler of my psyche, and it settled in comfortably and contently. Its plan was to reign indefinitely in my psyche; however, its rule was disrupted, in a rather unexpected way, when I challenged its power.

****

Cathy couldn't contain her excitement over the phone:

"Girl, I found the answer. I found the answer." She exclaimed this with such vagueness that I had to inquire.

"Found the answer to what?" I asked with great curiosity.

"The answer to our weight loss."

I don't know how it happened, but one day I woke up 30 pounds heavier than my ideal weight. Based on the Body Mass Index (the Body Mass Index or BMI is a measure of your body fat based on your weight and height), I was overweight. Never had I been overweight in my life. In fact, growing up, I was the tall, thin girl who always got teased about her skinny legs. At that time, I wished I were overweight. Nevertheless, with age, lack of exercise, unshed baby weight, and unlimited servings of fried chicken and fried anything, I became an overweight mother of four. Hoooohummm. Certainly, I tried to exercise and eat healthily. I even tried Weight Watchers, lemon diets, potato diets (don't remember what that was about), and all other kinds of diets. I wasn't successful on any of them (not to mention the fact that I didn't commit wholeheartedly to any). I'd start week one with a bang, but by week two, day three, I was back to my old ways. While I was excited along with Cathy about the prospect of losing weight (again), I wasn't too convinced that whatever this "new" weight-loss thingy was would actually work.

"Girl, it's a program called, 'Take Shape for Life.' We eat five meals per day."

I was listening attentively now.

"Oohhhh...wait, it says we eat five SMALL meals per day."

I was no longer listening attentively.

Cathy went on to explain something or other about this or that. I don't recall because I was half listening, until she said:

"And we can lose between two-five pounds per week![22]"
What??? Stop the happy press!! Did she say two-five pounds PER WEEK?

I asked, "Where can I get some of that?"

Cathy and I enrolled in the program in November 2010. She would be my coach, but we would lose weight together. For the next three months, we spoke three-four times per week about our progress. After the first week, I stepped on the scale and discovered that my weight was down five pounds! I couldn't believe it. I could actually see a hint of a waist appearing as I examined my body in the mirror. Before this program, I tried not to look at myself for too long in the mirror, because I never liked what I saw. I had a tendency to criticize what I saw.

With the help of Coach Cathy, week after week I dropped between two-five pounds. By February 2011, I shed 25 pounds. I marveled at how my body was changing right before my very eyes, and I was excited about my progress. Even more, I was proud that I had stuck to this program. There were many times during the program when I wanted to quit; however, I didn't want to disappoint Coach Cathy, nor myself. I felt powerful, as if I could do anything

I set my mind to do. While eating dinner one night, and observing that I had fixed my plate according to the protocol of ½ vegetables, ¼ protein, and ¼ complex carbohydrates, a thought occurred to me that I had never considered before: "If I can change my body by losing weight, and if I can do anything I set my mind to do, then maybe--just maybe--I can 'change' my greatest fear."

The opportunity to change my fear of open water winked at me just as the opportunity to lose weight did--unexpectedly. I saw a flyer for a women's triathlon entitled, "SheROX: She Swims, She Bikes, She Runs, SheROX." Hmmm…I could bike and I could run. But swim? That was my greatest fear. I could get in a pool, as long as I had the safety of the pool's side. This swim, however, would not be in a pool. It would be in the river. The swim distance for this triathlon was .33 miles, the bike ride was 15 miles, and it concluded with a 5K run. Before I would be able to participate in the triathlon, guess what I had to learn to do? Exactly! Swim! In the river! Which is entirely different than swimming in a pool!

Knowing I could not learn to river-swim on my own, I decided to collaborate with another SheROX participant. She invited me to join her at 7 a.m. at the boathouse along Philadelphia's Schuylkill River. There, I would be matched with an experienced rower who would monitor me as I swam in the river, to ensure my safety. When I arrived at the boathouse at 6:50 a.m., Celeste, my SheROX companion, introduced me to Steve and Sabrina. Sabrina would spot me as I swam in the river, and Steve would spot Celeste. I sat on the small dock, looking out on the river. She seemed so vast, so overwhelming. She beckoned me to come to her, to experience her. I heard her call me, just like she did at the San Pedro pier. But I wasn't ready to answer this time. Celeste said, "later," jumped into the river, and swam so far out that I could no longer see her or Steve in the distance. I remained on the dock, still looking out. That first day was so frightening for me that I couldn't remember the details. I asked Sabrina to share her recollection of what happened to me that day.

Here is her version:

> "I heard Celeste mention to Steve that some women training for the triathlon wanted to practice swimming in the river. She was hoping that Steve could be a spotter for what I initially imagined to be a group of five or six ladies. One spotter would be more than enough, but two spotters would be better. So, I offered my help for that first day and any following practices. My mouth watered at the idea that I would have extra time on the river. It never occurred to me that I was to be anything more than an extra pair of eyes.
>
> While driving to the club that morning, I could picture a handful of

competitive, athletic women, so ambitious to race that they would throw themselves in the river just to gain a small advantage over their fellow competitors come race day. They would be fit and fire-eyed dames who swore like sailors or reserved lionesses that pounced on a race when the gun was fired. I would be a side note to the affair - just a girl in a kayak floating by.

So when the pack of expected women thinned out to no more than the fearless Celeste and one other, I realized that I was extraneous. Two swimmers couldn't possibly need more than one spotter. But in my self-centered yearning to return to the water, I looked for a way to feel useful. It was then that I learned that the second swimmer was afraid of the water. A question popped into my head upon learning about this glitch: "Why would a woman, afraid of the open water, compete in a triathlon that includes an open water swim?" And then the answer came as fast as the question. "Why not!" There I was, standing before an individual who was epitomizing that which I hoped to achieve. She was inviting change into her life. She was living.

That first swim held nothing of what I originally planned. My morning of paddling on the river turned into kayak dog-paddling by the dock. My skin was itching to tear through the water. And yet, I was mesmerized by this lean, determined mother of four. Her hesitation to leap into the water caste her out of the fierce competitor image I had formed of the triathletes. Yet, her drive and competitive nature was clear. She wanted to win. She wanted that edge over her competitor. She was all in. The adjustment that I had to make in my perception of this athlete, however, lay in with whom she was competing against. For here before me was both the triathlete and her competitor in one. Race day was at hand on this first morning as the fear roared in her heart. Pam was up against herself.

At no point did I feel compelled to convince her to get into the water. She was not there to be a meek spirit needing coercion and praise. If anything, she needed patience and space to do exactly what she had determined would be done. Knowing how powerful and overwhelming fear can be, I tried to keep her mind from entrenching in the cyclical thoughts that breed panic. I made use of my ever-bizarre storage of factoids about how the brain processes things. And then, I pushed little by little for her to discover how far she would go that first day. Pam carefully studied the distance from the dock - where she remained glued -

to the collection of gigantic rocks peeking from the river floor 150 feet away. She mounted her red SheROX swim cap on her head and fitted her goggles onto her eyes. I could tell her heart was pounding. I could almost hear it. Methodically, with eyes on the rocks ahead, she put one foot in the river, followed by the second foot, and then her torso. She wasn't prepared for how warm the water felt and how murky it was too. Now committed to the water, she placed her head underneath and headed to the rocks. As she moved, so did I in the kayak. I was right by her side and she made sure I was. She struggled to get across, fighting it seemed. She called out to me as if I were far away. For a much-needed pause, she held on to the tip of the kayak, with eyes still focused on her destination. When she caught her breath, she put her head back under and headed for the rocks. I was right with her. She stopped again and again, repeating the same routine until finally she reached the rocks. Gasping for air, she pulled herself up onto the rocks and just sat there surveying the distance she had come, which seemed like an eternity. Then she realized the inevitable: she had to go back the same distance in order to get back to the dock! Once again she struggled and stopped, held on to the edge of the boat for a long time, and then struggled and stopped again and again on her way back. When she finally arrived at the dock, she grabbed on to the wood frame and held on as if for dear life. While little distance in nautical miles was covered, years of mental and emotional rewiring began.

No one does this - confronting fear head on. Seriously. Usually, when people do conquer a fear as strong as Pam's fear of the water, they write a book or make the circuit as inspirational speakers. It is that rare, it seems. We as humans find comfort in our surrender to our phobias. Hell, our loved ones cater to our fears, as the husband handles the mouse-traps for his wife and she in turn takes care of the elderly parents as they deteriorate. We organize our lives to avoid the confrontation of how an irrational thought or feeling brings us to our knees.

Pam pulled herself up onto the dock, visibly tired and visibly emotional. She was crying inconsolably. She had been so calm and clear in articulating what she could and could not do, that I was confused by the reason behind the tears. One minute, I'm telling her what an amazing accomplishment she had already made in getting in the water and swimming away from the dock, and the next minute, she is walking away from me in tears. Was *she disappointed at her progress? Was she deciding to never again dip herself into that nasty river water? Was she angry at her fear and herself for holding on to it all of these years? My curiosity was present enough to think those questions, but my respect for her had grown so that I understood that the questions were just as intimate as the answers were private. She walked to a bench a distance from the dock and continued sobbing. I sat with her, in silence. I understood she was having a private moment, yet I wanted her to know I was with her, in spirit. She finally spoke, stating what I already knew: she had just accomplished the remarkable. It wasn't the swimming from the dock to the rocks and back, but facing her fear. And I was honored to have participated in her transformation."*

Sabrina would coach me one more time before the actual day of the triathlon. That morning in October 2011, eight months after my weight loss success, when my alarm went off at 5 a.m., I thought of every reason not to show up. I didn't want to care and I didn't want to face the actual race, because practicing swimming 300 feet over and over again privately with a coach was nothing like swimming .33 miles with 100s of other women! Nevertheless, I geared up and headed to the race. I was in the wave of the slowest swimmers. The horn blew and there seemed to be a million women, all wearing red swim caps. I jumped in the river with them and started swimming for my life. However, I waded in the river until most had gone ahead. I had heard horror stories of women getting knocked on the head and then drowning because no one could see them in the sea of other competitive swimmers. I paced myself, keeping an eye on the first buoy in the far distance. If I could just get to the first one, I could hang on to it and rest.

I made it, rested, and set my sight on the next buoy. The river was so large, so overwhelming. I felt so small in it. I started to panic. Then I remembered something Sabrina told me during my training with her. She told me to make peace with the river and to see her as my friend, not my enemy. I began to talk to the river as I swam and told her how much I admired her strength. I talked to her until I got to the second buoy. Two more buoys to go and the finish-line would be in sight. By the time I got to the fourth buoy, I was becoming tired and scared. Would I be able to make it? I saw the large finish line banner far in the distance. I was about 500 feet away, yet it seemed miles away. I wasn't sure I would make it, and I started to cry inside. I felt my body fatiguing and panic starting to rise, just like at the San Pedro pier. Then out of nowhere, one of the spot swimmers came along my right side and said, "Hey, I'm going to swim the rest of the way with you, okay?" She was my angel, just like Sabrina was.

"Come on!" she encouraged, and all of a sudden, I had renewed energy. Stroke after stroke after stroke, I saw the finish line appear closer and closer. I looked over to make sure she was still with me. "I'm right here," she reminded me. I felt encouraged. My strokes became longer. "You're almost there! Keep going!," she announced. And I did keep going until I could finally feel the mushy sand beneath my feet. As I made my final stroke across the finish line, two men stepped into the bank, grabbed my arms, lifted me to my feet, and escorted me to the dry sand. I made it! I did it! I completed a .33 miles swim in the open water of the Philadelphia Schuylkill River. I conquered my fear and lived to share it. My life would never, ever be the same. I turned back towards the river to thank my Angel for swimming with me, but she was nowhere in sight.

As I approached the transition station to mount my bike, I broke down in tears, realizing what I had just accomplished. I thanked God for my Angel Swimmer and Sabrina, my Angel Coach. I only wished that Sabrina had been there to witness my accomplishment. The bike ride was the easiest and most pleasant 15-mile ride I ever had. As I biked, I waved to the other bikers, gave thumbs up signs to the supporters, and sang happy songs to myself. Back at the transition station, I parked my bike and put on my running shoes. I was now on the last phase of my triathlon: two down and one to go. Naturally, I was tired. By mile 2.5, I was ready to quit and just sit on the curb and go to sleep. I kept going because I didn't want to embarrass myself. After all, my family was waiting for me at the finish line, somewhere. At about mile 2.75, I heard a voice call out to me, "Go, Pam! Go!!!" It was a familiar voice, and it seemed to be following me as I ran. I couldn't spot the person behind the voice, so I kept running. And, the voice kept following me. When I looked over to my right, guess who was running on the pavement alongside me while I ran in the street? Sabrina!! My Angel Coach found me in the crowd of hundreds of runners and was there to get me to the finish line. "Go, Pam! Go!" she rooted me on. I felt the wind beneath my wings because Sabrina was there with me. I picked up my pace and as I saw the finish line ahead of me, I bolted! I crossed the finish line strongly and confidently, and with much rejoicing. I, Pamela Elaine Nichols, had completed my first women's triathlon, SheROX. The following year, 2012, I participated for the second time in SheROX, and you know what? I ROCK!!!

Fear was no longer my lord. It was now my servant.

Oh and by the way, my companion, Celeste? Well, she won first place for completing the triathlon in her age group. Go Celeste!

LESSON APPLICATION

Have you ever experienced fear many, many times? All of us have. Fear is a normal biological process that has one purpose: protection. What is fear? According to Discovery Channel's website[23]:

> *"Fear is a series of reactions in the brain triggered by a stressful stimulus and ending with such physical reactions as tense muscles, rapid heartbeat and rushed breathing. This is the well-known fight-or-flight response. Examples of fear stimuli include stage fright, spiders, seeing someone attacking with a knife or the sound of the front door suddenly banging open."*

This response is automatic. It's not something you think about, process, and then respond to. Self-protection and self-preservation are in your DNA. The problem with fear is that what is a biological process meant for protection becomes a barrier to growth. You become paralyzed by a repeated fear and get stuck in it. In other words, the problem with repeated fear is that it lies to you and you keep listening. It rules you, and you obey.

Overcoming your repeated fear is a process that requires intention, time, and attention. You may not overcome your fear in one day or with one effort. However, with commitment and consistency, you can overcome your fear and no longer be ruled by it.

From my experience, and with help from research, I offer you five simple steps to claim victory over your fear:

> **Step 1: Name it** - What is the name of your fear? Speaking, heights, open water, dying, spiders, losing a loved one, etc.?

> **Step 2: Own it** – Acknowledge that you have this fear, that you repeat the fear over and over again in your mind, and that it lives with you. Ownership does not mean weakness or something bad. You cannot overcome something you don't admit exists.

> **Step 3: Know it** - Understand what this fear is all about. Come to

realize from where it originated, how it manifests in your life, and what it truly represents. Study its effects on you like you would an important exam. Know where the fear shows up in your body (gut, chest, shoulders, etc.).

Step 4: Risk it - Risk facing your fear. Write down all the possibilities your life could be like if you didn't have this repeated fear. Then, share these possibilities with another person. It will take effort just to share your fear because fear keeps us silent too. Repeated fear does not want to be exposed. Invite this person to support you in facing your fear.

Step 5: Dethrone it – Take a specific action in the possibility you wrote down and have the person you shared it with support you here too. Celeste and Sabrina (and my Angel Swimmer) supported me in dethroning my fear.

This will take practice. Don't worry, however. Some fears will be easy to face while others will be difficult. Whether easy or difficult, you can face your fear and have victory over it. And victory is oh, so sweet!

YOUR TURN

Name it, Own it, Know it, Risk it, Dethrone it. What's your fear?

_____

_____

_____

_____

_____

"Weeping may endure for a night, but joy comes in the morning."

- Psalm 30:5

LESSON

8

Joy Is A Healing Soil.

I was in the kitchen washing dishes while I kept an eye on the clock. Soon it would be time to pick the kids up from school. The phone rang, disrupting my cleaning rhythm. "Hello?" My sister-in-law's voice was on the other end. She was not one for small talk; so, after the requisite, "Hello. How are you and the family?" questions, she got right to the purpose of her call.

"Pam, I know what depression looks like. You are depressed, and you need help."

She said these words with gentleness and respect, but I was stunned at her pronouncement. For though she and I were cordial and enjoyed one another's company, we were not particularly close. I didn't know her well, nor did she really know me. And even if she did know me, I thought I did an exceptional job pretending that I was happy and that my life was perfect.

As she went on to explain why she thought I was depressed, my mind went back to the day we had a rare and candid conversation over lunch. Before she returned to her home in up-state New York, I drove her to her connecting destination. We stopped for a bite to eat. During our lunch, she confronted me about a sadness she perceived that I was carrying—a sadness that I was hiding. She told me that I didn't let anyone into my pain. Now, she and I didn't hang out regularly. As I mentioned, we rarely saw each other. Yet somehow, she knew me at a deeper level than just the surface. Surprised at her insight and desperate to let someone in on my secret, I told her about my private pain of being a wife and mother, having uncertainty about my purpose in life, and not being financially self-sufficient. I talked to her about the fact that I hated my life. She listened carefully and encouraged constructively. We finished lunch and I drove her to her connection, thinking that our lovely little conversation would never happen again...until I received her phone call.

I was a functional depressive. Meaning, I did all the tasks a wife and mother "should" do, never missing a beat. Some days I was happy. Many days I was not. Most days, however, one would never know the difference. I knew how to pretend because acting was my greatest accomplishment in high school! As a member of the Thespian Society in high school, I earned the lead part in most of the plays I performed in. For three consecutive years, I won "Best Actress" awards for my performances. I knew so well how to keep up a front - a best performing act - that I came to believe my act was my truth.

My sister-in-law was right. I was depressed. I couldn't fake it any longer, at least not with her. The reasons for my depression were numerous, yet there was a specific root cause. Getting to the root cause took patience, time, energy, and an open mind. An open mind means a willingness to ask difficult questions and to seek professional help. I did both. Dealing with depression is not like going to a fast food restaurant. It is a methodical process that requires persistence, belief in the process, and commitment in order to overcome it.

The root of my depression was my basic belief that I WAS NOT GOOD ENOUGH! I ate, drank, bathed, and slept in this belief. I wasn't good enough to express what I wanted. I wasn't good enough to ask, unapologetically, for what I needed. I wasn't good enough to live a life that made me happy. I wasn't good enough to admit how unhappy I really was. I wasn't good enough for my voice to be heard, honored, and validated. I wasn't good enough to hold to my beliefs when others disagreed. I wasn't good enough to be loved by my Grandmother the way she seemed to love my sister. I wasn't good enough for my elementary school best friend to believe me over the lies of another classmate. I wasn't good enough for my first husband to stay married to me. I wasn't good enough for my parents to stay married to each other. I wasn't good enough for my father to remain faithful to my mother. I wasn't good enough for my teenage crush to choose me over the girl who offered him sex. I wasn't good enough for my relative to protect me, but to instead help my neighbor pull down my panties to look at my private parts. I wasn't good enough for my sister and brother to invite me to their fun events together. I wasn't good enough. I wasn't good enough. I just wasn't good enough! Everything I did in life was based on this fundamental belief that I was not good enough.

My sister-in-law's phone call was my lifesaver. Her statement challenged me to look at the manifestation of depression in my life. Weeks after her call, I sought the help of a therapist. I began to see how my "not good enough" perception clouded my perspective, decisions, relationships, and behavior. My "not good enough" belief had much to do with keeping up my pretense too. My therapist helped guide me to the root cause of my depression. With skill and commitment, she helped me understand that depression could be replanted in the soil of my choosing. Years of counseling, self-reflection, forgiveness (of myself and others), and words of affirmation from family and friends enabled me to accept the truth that I AM good enough – just as I am - and to find joy in that truth. Slowly, I began to replant the seeds of depression in a soil of my choosing – joy! Oh, and what a fully fragrant flower I have bloomed into.

LESSON APPLICATION

Joy! Oh, joy!

Joy is defined as the emotion evoked by well-being, success, or good fortune, or by the prospect of possessing what one desires. (Merriam-Webster)

Doesn't just reading that definition evoke JOY within you? I hope so. Joy is our natural state as human beings. Depression, the enemy of joy, is not our natural state. You were created to experience joy in this life. Dr. Christiane Northrup, a renowned obstetrician and gynecologist and best-selling author, explains why joy is indeed our natural state. In her audiobook, "The Power of Joy", she makes the case for joy as our natural state in this way:

> *Life is meant to be joyous! We are pleasure-seeking creatures by nature. Joy makes you younger, smarter, more intuitive, and healthier . . . with better hormonal balance and immune-system functioning. Joy even positively affects your metabolism.*[24]

Dr. Northrup further explains that every time we feel joy, a chemical called nitric oxide is released from the lining of our blood vessels (called endothelium). Nitric oxide results in an increase of blood flow throughout the body. The flow of blood is the flow of joy and delight!

The benefits of joy are numerous, as she points out:

1. It brings out the best in you.
2. It makes you younger.
3. It increases the youth hormone (DHEA or Dehydroepiandrosterone)[25]
4. It enhances your immunity.
5. It changes your metabolism.
6. It creates success.
7. It enhances creativity and intuition.
8. It makes you irresistible.
9. It decreases stress hormones.

Yet, we don't trust joy. We are suspicious of it, although we crave its satisfaction daily and in many forms (whether beneficial or not): eating, drinking, sugar consumption, entertainment, drugs and alcohol, sex, etc. Imagine the distrust you might have of a co-worker who comes to work daily with a joyful attitude. Wouldn't you be a bit suspicious of her? You might think she is faking. You might even think she smokes something or pops pills, because NO ONE can have that much joy everyday! And, when we do experience joy, we either feel guilty or worry that something terrible will happen and wipe the joy right off our faces.

But how do we find joy? How do we experience joy on a daily basis? The answer is, *intend it*! Intend it. With your intention, you can evoke joy into your life. Intention is that which you plan to do or achieve. It's an aim or purpose. Intention is formed in your thoughts, and thoughts have creative power. According to the National Science Foundation[26], researchers have reported that our brains produce 50,000 thoughts per day. Neuroscientists and psychologists say 90% of these are negative and repetitive and 99% are a gross misrepresentation of reality or are unreliable. Thoughts can be measured using MRI (magnetic resonance imaging) and have an effect on the chemical structure of the cells in our body. These chemical changes in the body can be measured as well.

In a fascinating article in PsychologyToday.com, the author of "Depression Doing the Thinking: Take Action Right Now to Convert Negative to Positive Thinking[27]", Hara Estroff Marano, writes:

One of the features of depression is pessimistic thinking. The negative thinking is actually the depression speaking. It's what depression sounds like. Depression in fact manifests in negative thinking before it creates negative affect.

Most depressed people are not aware that the despair and hopelessness they feel are flowing from their negative thoughts. Thoughts are mistakenly seen as privileged, occupying a rarefied territory, immune to being affected by mood and feelings, and therefore representing some immutable truth.

As I began to understand the root of my depression (that my beliefs, which were being created by my thoughts, were running the show), I focused my intention on my healing. I fixated my thoughts on healing and began seeking resources that could help in the healing process. As I mentioned, I sought qualified, professional help. In addition, resources such as Dr. Northrup's audiobook mysteriously dropped into my path, as if knocked off the shelf right in front of my feet by some invisible force. I have listened to Dr. Northrup's audiobook at least a dozen times. It reminds me that when I find myself backsliding into negative feelings, I must check my thoughts and ask, "What am I thinking?" Sure enough, my thoughts are somewhere fighting in a dark alley. In the moments of the fighting, I have a choice to make: to change my negative thoughts to positive ones and experience joy that follows or die bloodied on the ground. More specifically, I do the following:

1. I play my favorite songs that make me feel good and start singing. My children look at me strangely (and ask me to please be quiet) as I sing loudly and dance around the house.

2. I read my favorite inspirational quotes.

3. I write in my gratitude journal.

4. I call one of my best friends, who is funny as heck, for a hearty, joyous laugh.

5. I affirm myself by listing as many things that I like about myself as I can stand (Dr. Northrop states that affirmations don't make something happen, they make something welcome. Welcome joy. Welcome peace. Welcome happiness. Welcome whatever you want).

6. I walk on the grass barefoot.

7. I meditate.

8. I go for a 5-mile run, knowing that when I'm finished, my body will enjoy the release of stress!

The point of this list is to help you become aware of your thoughts, or, to become "mindful." Being mindful means creating an opportunity to transform your negative thoughts (depressing, "not good enough") into joyous thoughts ("You are fabulous and so is life").

Replanting the seeds of depression, or any other negative disposition, into the soil of joy is a conscious, intentional practice. For someone like me, who became comfortable with feeling depressed, learning this lesson became my life-line. And when you replant in the soil of joy, that negative disposition will begin to dissipate.

Certainly, you will experience depression, hurt, disappointment, sadness, loss, feelings of powerlessness, etc. These experiences are part of life. But they don't have to become permanently rooted or define who you are. When you experience them, remember what your natural state is: JOY.

Happy replanting!

YOUR TURN

If joy is your natural state, what is hindering you from replanting your negative feelings into the soil of joy? What is one action you can take right now to replace negative thoughts with joyful thoughts?

_____

_____

_____

_____

_____

_____

> *"When you want something, all the universe conspires in helping you to achieve it."*
>
> *- from* <u>The Alchemist</u> *by Paulo Coelho*

LESSON

9

Wants Matter!

I stumbled into the realization that wants hold creative power. The realization began rather innocently...well...not exactly. It began when I recognized how upset I became every time my middle child (I'll call her Daughter 2) would not listen to my instructions and, would instead, do the opposite. Accompanying every opposite action was her standard response when asked "why" she did not follow my instructions. Her standard response would send me into such a tailspin that I had no other choice but to examine why it did.

For example, after 7 p.m., Daughter 2 was not allowed to drink any liquids. Being at the tender age when bed-wetting was typical, I did not want to be the one cleaning up the mess, yet again. My instructions to her were clear:

"It's almost bedtime. Remember, no juice after 7 p.m., okay?"

"Okay, mommy." She responded, compliantly.

The next morning when it was time for me to wake her for school, I noticed that her sheets were wet. Frustrated and suspicious, I asked:

"Daughter 2, did you drink juice after 7 p.m. when I told you not to?"

With innocence and simplicity her response was, "Yes, mommy."

"Why, when I told you no juice after 7 p.m.?" I shot back, feeling my blood start to boil.

Without fail, her standard response effortlessly flowed from her lips: "Because I wanted to." No attitude. No back-talk. She replied quietly and respectfully.

My standard reaction: Begin tailspin. Start lecture.

"Just because you WANTED to does not give you a reason to disobey my orders. You cannot do something just because you WANT to! Do you UNDERSTAND??????"

Apologetically, she replied, "Yes, mommy."

Thinking to myself, "lesson learned," I eased my tension, calmed my nerves, pivoted, and walked out of her room. Until, of course, she disobeyed my instructions again. This time it wasn't juice; it was her room.

I sent her to clean the mess of a room she constantly kept, reminding her that I planned to check it in 45 minutes. True to my word, 45 minutes later I was at her bedroom door…fuming.

"Daughter 2, didn't I tell you to clean your room?"

"Yes, mommy" she politely responded.

"And instead, you are playing with dolls and your room is still a mess!! Can you tell me why you are playing when I told you to clean up?"

Quietly and respectfully she replied, "Because I wanted to." No attitude. No back-talk.

Smoke bellowed from the top of my head. Everything in me wanted to spank her butt.

Again, my standard reaction: Begin tailspin. Start lecture.

"Just because you WANTED to does not give you a reason to disobey my orders. You cannot do something just because you WANT to? Do you UNDERSTAND??????"

Apologetically, she replied, "Yes, mommy."

My thinking was this: If I repeated the "wants-don't-matter" lecture enough times, she would get the message. But, she didn't, and it wasn't long before I corrected the same behavior again, and again, and again.

Her disobedience to my instructions was not the primary reason I got so angry with her. Instead, it was her reason ("because I wanted to") for the disobedience that caused a visceral reaction within me. I had to know why. Why was I so angry and frustrated with her **reason**? Why did I hate that reason so much? I didn't have an immediate answer; however, soon enough, the answer would evolve.

******

One afternoon, when I was in a rush to quickly get in and out of the grocery store, then back home in time to pick my children up from school, a thought occurred to me as I pulled into the parking lot. I verbalized that thought aloud, to myself: "I want a parking space next to the entrance." As I drove my car down one parking isle that was closest to the entrance, low and behold, there was a spot open when all the other spots were taken. I got out of the car (thankful that I was so lucky), did my shopping, and made it home in time to pick my kids up from school.

Several days later, I was in another grocery-store-rush. This time I was at a different store. I said aloud to myself again, "I sure want a parking space next to the entrance." As I cruised down the parking isle closest to the entrance, I saw NO empty spaces. Suddenly, I slammed on my breaks. A car was backing out of the space right in front of me. I didn't even see the car or the driver get into it. "Wow! Lucky me," I thought. I went inside, did my shopping, and went about my business.

The third, fourth, fifth, sixth, and seventh time, the same thing happened. I said aloud to myself that I wanted a parking space near the entrance. Then, no more than two minutes later, a spot became available. By the seventh time, I had an epiphany: "What if I am creating openings simply by WANTING a parking space near the entrance?" Curious, I decided to test my hypothesis by following these steps:

1. I determined in advance where I wanted a parking space.
2. I pulled my car into the exact isle where I wanted a parking space.
3. I decided which side of the isle I wanted to park (sometimes

left, sometimes right. Either way, I chose one).
4. I turned on my blinker and waited, with expectation.

Ninety percent of the time, a spot was already open or was becoming available because someone was backing out. Usually, I never saw the person get in the car beforehand. All I know is that a car was backing out of the space, on the side of the isle in which I wanted to park. Ten percent of the time, I had to wait one-two minutes. That was a short time to wait for what I wanted.

I thought I was crazy! How can this be happening not once, not twice, but consistently? Just to make sure I wasn't crazy, I took my kids shopping with me one day. On the way, I announced to them, "Hey kids, I can create a parking space anywhere I want to!" I was shaking in my boots because kids can make you feel like such a fool. They laughed and said, "Yeah right, Mom!" While they were in the car, I said, "I want a parking spot in this isle and on my right side." We were at the Apple store, where parking was always very limited, and people drove frantically around and around for a parking spot. I didn't. I pulled to the side so other cars that were driving in circles could pass me, turned on my blinker, and waited. In less than one minute, a guy came out of the Apple store, walked right to the same place where I was waiting, got into his car, and drove off. I pulled into MY spot (that he was holding for me) with a big, fat "I told you so" smile. My kids grumbled because to them, waiting one minute was too long. They were not impressed and grumbled while exiting the car. I repeated this with my kids in the car on three different occasions! By the third time, they became convinced.

I began to notice something strangely familiar. I noticed that my wants drove my behavior, and my behavior, caused a visible effect. How could this effect originate from a simple (even trivial) want? My mind swung back around to my numerous lectures to Daughter 2 regarding her wants and why they didn't matter. Perhaps my visceral reaction to her disobedience toward me in order to honor her wants was a sign...a message. The message could be that wants actually DO matter. Perhaps the God of the Universe wanted me to learn a valuable lesson, a lesson that would change how I parent and how I honor myself. The unrest I felt every time Daughter 2 responded with, "Because I wanted to," was unrest for an important reason.

I also learned that my wants are important simply because I, Pamela Elaine, am important. Whether my wants are trivial (parking space) or significant (a better relationship with my children), my wants matter! From the moment I understood this lesson, I have begun to listen to and honor my wants, no matter what they are. If I want to spend time alone when my children would rather I engage them, I spend time alone. When I feel renewed, I engage them.

When I want to sleep those extra 30 minutes, I do. I rearrange my schedule to accommodate that extra 30 minutes. When I want to go out for a pleasant evening of dinner and a movie, and there is no one available to go with me, I take myself and enjoy my own company! Honoring my wants has made me a happy, self-confident woman. And, a happy, self-confident woman is a treasure.

LESSON APPLICATION

My wants invoked a law that I wasn't even aware existed. Daughter 2 indirectly revealed not only the power of attraction that our wants have but also why they matter. She inadvertently led me to the Law of Attraction.

In her book, The Secret[28], written by Rhonda Byrne, several expert practitioners of the Law of Attraction spell out exactly what this law is. The experts in The Secret report that as we think and feel, a corresponding frequency is set out into the universe that attracts back to us events and circumstances on that same frequency. These practitioners state that when we are positive in our outlook on our situation and circumstances, then we position ourselves to attract positive people and positive situations and circumstances. Conversely, when we are negative or angry in our outlook, then we tend to attract the same kind of people and circumstances: negative and angry. You attract the predominant thought that you are holding in your awareness, whether those thoughts are in your conscious or unconscious mind.

This was a challenge for me to accept as I thought about many unwanted circumstances in my life and in the lives of others. The practitioners challenge the reader to consider the Law of Gravity, as a comparison. The Law of Gravity does not care if you are conscious or unconscious of its existence. If you jump off the top of a building, you are going to hit the ground! It doesn't matter if you are a good or a bad person. It doesn't matter if you are aware or unaware.

Universal laws (or laws of nature) are impartial and have no favorites. Just as importantly, these laws are not forgiving if you are ignorant of them. Ignore them and die (emotionally, spiritually, physically, financially). Respect them and live.

What you want (and what you don't want) influence your thoughts. Your thoughts influence your feelings. According to quantum physicists, thoughts have energy that can be measured. Energy is a creative force. In other words, what you want (or don't want) influences your thoughts and your thoughts influence your feelings. If you ever want to know what you are feeling, ask yourself what you are thinking. Experts say your thoughts cause your circumstances (or the life you are experiencing) or your reality--a reality that YOU have created.

I struggled with this concept. Many questions, which I am sure you are asking yourself too, formulated in my mind. Immediately, I thought about the terrible, unnecessary tragedies in the world. Did thoughts create these events? I don't completely understand this law. Perhaps that's not required right now. As with many laws, careful examination is necessary in order to fully explain them. However, based on what I have experienced in my life and have witnessed in the lives of so many I know and have coached, there is something notable about this law. While scientists were still trying to understand gravity and devise mathematical equations for it, once they understood that "jumping off buildings" could end your life, they ceased this behavior as they better prepared to explain the law more precisely. Now we live in a world where the Law of Gravity is better understood and respected.

We might still have some distance to go in understanding and systematizing the Law of Attraction. For now, it's worthwhile to be attentive to our wants, the feelings these wants engender, and the thoughts that follow.

Side Note

Back to Daughter 2 and the lesson she taught me. Whenever you have a strong reaction to something, anything, pay attention to it. Pay close attention if you constantly have the same strong reaction to that same "something." There is a lesson in the reaction. A simple self-analysis to help you uncover the lesson is as follows: Identify, Ask, and Determine.

1. **IDENTIFY** the immediate and specific feeling that follows the event/circumstance by completing the following sentence: "Right now, I am feeling _____ by this event/circumstance, although what I might really be feeling is _____."
2. **ASK** yourself "why" you are feeling this way and let your answer

focus on you rather than place blame on someone else for making you feel what you are feeling: "I am feeling this way because I _____."

3. **DETERMINE** the positive lesson this feeling may be teaching you by completing the following sentence: "This feeling may be teaching me _____."

Specifically, my daughter's constant reply, "Because I wanted to" would blow a fuse in my head every time. I conducted my own self-analysis: IDENTIFY, ASK, and DETERMINE:

1. "Right now, I am feeling **PISSED OFF** by Daughter 2's disobedience, although what I might really be feeling is **JEALOUSY** that my daughter has the nerve to give me a lame excuse of 'because I wanted to' when I wouldn't have dared say such a thing to my parents."

2. "I am feeling JEALOUS because **I DIDN'T FEEL MY WANTS WERE HEARD AS A CHILD AND INSTEAD I BURIED THEM IN DEFERENCE TO MY PARENTS' AUTHORITY.**"

3. "This feeling may be teaching me that what I **WANT MATTERS.**"

YOUR TURN

Think about something you really, really, really want that could make you happy? Without assigning blame to anyone else, but instead taking full responsibility for your want, what's keeping you from having it?

_____

_____

_____

_____

> *" . . . For the Lord sees not as man sees: man looks on the outward appearance, but the Lord looks on the heart."*
>
> *- 1 Samuel 16:7 ESV*

LESSON

10

Authenticity Transforms Contention Into Closeness.

Have you ever wanted to pop your child upside his head? I know that sounds harsh, but I'm serious. Have you? Well, I wanted to...at rapid-fire speed! I was fed up with my son's bad attitude toward me, day after day. His behavior had become arrogant, defiant, and disruptive to his sisters and me. If I said, "The sky is blue," he would quip, "How do you even know there IS a sky?" If I said, "Please go clean your room," he would respond, "Why do I have to do that now?" It seemed that no matter what I said or told him to do, both his attitude and his mouth equated to an annoying experience for me. One evening, after yet another contentious exchange between us, I made a decision. Instead of popping him on his head, as I wanted to do dozens of times before, I posted the following request in a private group on Facebook:

> *"Would really appreciate recommendations for books/videos/ therapists/wizards to help me understand how to manage adolescents who lose their minds before I put my seventh grader out on the streets. Thank you."*

Many responded with concrete advice...and others with more humorous advice, such as, "Read the book, The Rollercoaster Years and, Get Out of My

Life, but First Could You Drive Me & Cheryl to the Mall: A Parent's Guide to the New Teenager." Other suggestions included reading an article in www. AhaParenting.com, taking him to see a therapist, and not speaking to him. Others advised me to put him out of the house for awhile, act as though I also lost my mind on him, or get in the car, drive two blocks from the house, and sit there until they freak out and start calling you, while you ignore them, then wait some more. I was even told that a glass of wine (or something stronger) also helps. One person even wrote, "I don't condone child abuse, but I certainly understand what turns Mr. Hand into Mr. Fist." This advice brought me comfort and chuckles. There was one suggestion, however, that rose above the crowd of advice because it offered an entirely different perspective. The advice came from an acquaintance I met, and after several dinners together and conversation, I had grown fond of her. Susan replied: "You need The Landmark Forum." I thought, "The Landmark who?" Never having heard of The Landmark Forum, and needing a quick fix to deal with my son's chronic bad temper and disrespectful attitude towards me, I picked up two of the recommended books at the library (which I never read), and called a therapist.

Months later, while out together sipping on sour apple martinis, Susan shared more with me about The Landmark Forum (Although I introduced The Landmark Forum in Lesson 4, this experience with Susan was my first time hearing about The Landmark Forum). As I shared in Lesson 4, Landmark's model is ontological, which they explain basically means their programs involve inquiring into the nature and function of being for human beings. The model - rather than providing theories or hypotheticals - provides direct access to what shapes and limits people's day to day lives, and opens up new possibilities for effectiveness and quality of one's life. (Huh???). Susan described how inquiring into her way of being (her thoughts, feelings, beliefs and interactions with others) had improved her relationships and empowered her with tools to live a life of her choosing, of her creation. I DID NOT GET IT. I was still confused...it seemed too abstract, non-scientific and downright hokey. Yet, I was open because I was at my wits end as a mother to an only boy with three sisters. Susan, being a thoughtful woman, a lawyer by training, and a business owner, didn't seem the type to dabble in hokey pokey-ness. I trusted that she knew what she was talking about. The following month, with Susan's financial contribution to my tuition, I enrolled in The Landmark Forum, having absolutely no concrete idea of what I was getting myself into.

On its website, Landmark Worldwide (the legal entity of The Landmark Forum) states: "Landmark Worldwide is an international personal and professional growth, training and development company—a global educational enterprise committed to the fundamental principle that people have the possibility of success, fulfillment and greatness."

Landmark offers a number of courses, one of which is The Landmark Forum. From the website, it describes the course as follows: a course "designed to bring about positive, permanent shifts in the quality of your life—in just three and a half days." That is really a short (even unrealistic) period of time to do the big work of "transformation." After all, "transformation" takes time, and much of it. Transformation takes decades. No, transformation takes a life-time! To me, 3 ½ days seemed an overpromise, and I was pissed off big-time with the overpromise the morning I sat my buns in my seat on the first day of the 3 ½-day course.

Yet, in that short time, something within my emotions shifted. I can't quantify the shift. I can only qualify it. During the course, I learned about a breakthrough concept called "authenticity." The course instructor stated over and over again what was to me a foreign concept: "Whenever you experience a loss of power, freedom, or self-expression, you must consider where you have been inauthentic." This was the most significant concept for me because I experienced a loss of power, self-expression and freedom with my son (not to mention with other relationships) daily! Specifically, being inauthentic – as the course teaches - means that I was pretending one way while in reality I felt another. In other words, being inauthentic costs something of value to all human beings (that is, power, freedom, or self-expression), particularly in relationships. On the other hand, authenticity brings power, self-expression, and freedom. Going deeper, authenticity in relationships brings intimacy, happiness, peace, and comfort (none of which I had in my relationship with my son). This lesson was so eye-opening for me, that on day two, while driving home in my car, I called each one of my children and shared ways I had been inauthentic with them. I asked their forgiveness. I even called my former spouse. I was surprised by how easy it was to call each one of my children and my former spouse and confess my areas of inauthenticity. I was just that liberated from the experience of the course.

The conversation with my son was the shortest, but most moving and inspiring.

"Hi Son. Can I talk to you for a moment?"

Politely and slowly, he answered, "Yeeess."

"I'm taking a class that is teaching me something important. Can I share it with you?"

Again, politely and slowly, he answered, "Yeeess."

"I have been pretending that you are not a smart boy and treating you like you are not, when in reality you are smart beyond your years. I want to know if you will forgive me and if we can share more time, with more hugs and kisses? Is that alright?"

His response lightened my heart and my eyes welled with tears. He responded as though he had heard the best news of his day, "YEAAHHSSSSS!" His enthusiasm filled my car. I felt his energy and good feelings.

Academic strength is something I value, and my daughters excel academically, consistently earning good grades. My son, on the other hand, does not earn those same high marks consistently. In fact, he struggles, comparatively. However, my son is smart beyond his years outside the realm of academics. He is a very emotionally-intuitive child, and is therefore spot-on when it comes to understanding the hidden thoughts and intentions of others. Where some adults are unable to, he is able to identify his feelings and motives and self-correct his course of action. He can smell pretention ten miles away. His ability often made me feel uncomfortable because he could point out my pretention when I thought I was being real. I didn't like the fact that he could identify those times I was being pretentious. Instead of accepting him and his ability, I rejected both. My distant and contentious feelings toward him faded in that brief phone call. It faded in a way that I am unable to pinpoint, but in an instant, it was gone.

However, that distant feeling didn't remain gone forever. Inevitably, he and I would clash again and again. With each clash, however, I had an opportunity to either apply what I learned about authenticity, or respond in my default fashion, which was to pretend I felt one way, when in reality I felt another. One way in which I pretend is to act as though I am his boss and he my employee (AKA, "do what I say or get fired!"). When I make this choice, distance between us grows. However, when I choose authenticity, we (re)connect! I have marveled at the power of being real.

Regularly, I continue to implement other breakthrough methods learned from The Landmark Forum. I continue to gain an understanding of what I learned about myself and how my relationship with myself influences my interactions with others, including my son. In that short, 3 ½ days, I found The Landmark Forum's teachings so compelling and useful in my day-to-day interactions, that I wanted more of it. I continually shared with my children what I was learning and how it applied to life, happiness, and relationships. In fact, I took them twice to sample the course during one of the introductory sessions. They enjoyed what they learned and wanted to attend the special 3 ½ -day program called "The Landmark Forum for Young People."

As part of the course package, participants of the The Landmark Forum are entitled to attend one ten-session series. Two weeks after completing the course, the first day of my ten-session series had come. That morning, I was super excited as I got the kids ready for school. I couldn't stop chattering to them about the ten-session seminar series I was about to take.

"Kids, this evening is the first day of the new program. I will pick you guys up from school, we'll head to the library to finish homework, and then head to dinner across the street from the seminar. You guys get to come with me into the seminar for a bit, then go to a spot to do your homework. Remember how much you enjoyed going with me the first and second time? Remember how much you learned and how excited you were to take your own course?" All of them remembered and shared their stories of what they had learned. I could hardly wait, and the kids could see my excitement. I'm usually not that excited about stuff around them (too busy with the details of completing tasks), so my happy, high-level energy was a treat for them to see.

During dinner, I introduced my kids to many of the participants that I came to know and love during the 3 ½ - day course. Since I talked so often to the participants about my kids during the course, they felt as though they already knew my kids pretty well. As the other participants, my children, and I packed tightly into the elevator to head to the Seminar, we chatted, hugged, and greeted one another more. The reunion energy was high and enthusiasm filled the elevator.

The plan went exactly as I imagined...until the unexpected happened. As we exited the elevator together and approached the check-in table, I noticed a peculiar look on the face of the seminar coordinator. He looked nervous.

> "Hi! Is there some place where my children can do their homework, while I attend the seminar?" I asked.

My kids and I huddled around the seminar coordinator, eagerly awaiting his direction to a cozy spot for them to work. Not sure how to respond, he said,

> "Uhhh…talk to Anthony. Ask him."

My kids and I walked over to Anthony and huddled around him the same way we did with the coordinator.

> "Hi! Is there some place where my children can do their activities while I attend the seminar?" I asked bright-eyed and bushy-tailed.

To my utter surprise, Anthony responded, emphatically and respectfully,

"No! There isn't." I thought he was kidding, so I asked again. And, he repeated again, "No! There isn't. I'm sorry. Children are not allowed in this building while we are in the seminar. They are a liability."

"A what?????" I couldn't believe what I was hearing. He went on to explain, recognizing that I had no idea children cannot be accommodated.

"We informed The Landmark Forum participants at enrollment of the seminar that children aren't allowed. Is there someone nearby you could call to watch the kids? Perhaps a friend? Their father?"

He went on and on, trying to be helpful, but actually I was so stunned that I couldn't hear what he was saying. I thought for a moment about whom I could dump four kids on at the 11th hour, and until 10:30p.m.! Alas, I could think of no one and sadly replied,

"Then I can't stay. I'll have to miss Day One of the seminar. There is no one who can watch my kids on such short notice."

What was wrong with missing the first day? After all, couldn't I just return for week two and catch whatever I missed in week one? No. The policy is you must attend the first session. Attendance at session one is mandatory. I didn't mention this part to the kids.

My children saw the sadness and disappointment on my face. I gathered my bags and we walked back to the elevator and out of the building. On our way out, I made a few phone calls to friends whom I thought might be able to watch the kids. No luck. My kids started offering suggestions of people to call, but none of their suggestions could be taken seriously ("Mr. Rabbit" doesn't watch kids...at least not anymore.) They even suggested that they babysit one another, alone. That wasn't a good idea either. In that moment, I hate to say, I wished my kids lived on a different planet. Not only did I feel they were the cause of my missing the next important step in my transformation, but I spent nearly $100 on dinner with them (and they didn't even eat half of their food!), and overpaid to park by $13 because the stupid Philadelphia city meter played a dirty trick on me. In one evening, I had spent over $120 and was not going to be able to conclude it with new learning and another profound experience. I wanted to cry.

As my children and I took a solemn, long five-minute walk back to where I had over-paid for parking, my youngest daughter grabbed my hand to hold it. My other daughters said they were sorry for me and expressed their sentiments. My son, however, was silent. We loaded into the car, and in somber silence, we rode home. No one talked. My disappointment was so thick, even a Cutco® Cutlery knife couldn't cut it. Twenty minutes later, and about five minutes from the house, my son, who was sitting in the front passenger's seat broke his silence:

"Mommy...when is your thing again?"

"What 'thing' do you mean, Son?" I asked quietly, not really in the mood for conversation or to figure out what he might be trying to ask.

"Your class. What day is it next time"?

"Monday...next Monday." I lied, knowing I had forfeited the entire ten-week seminar by missing the first class.

"Okay, then next Monday, Mommy, we will plan to go to a friend's house, or ask dad if he can watch us, or whatever we have to do so that you don't miss your class again because of us. Right guys?"

In that instant, my son rose out of the sad silence and did so with an authentic expression from his heart, which deeply touched my heart. Is this the same son who gives me a big fat headache? Who challenges me on every turn? Who gets an attitude with me at the drop of a hat? In that very moment, my feeling of distance towards him once again disappeared.

My old way of being was to have blamed Anthony, The Landmark Forum supervisor, for not making some accommodation for my children. However, through the transformation I experienced through The Landmark Forum teachings, I understood that I was "cause in the matter" of my experience. In other words, I was responsible for not being able to attend the first session and my kids not enjoying an evening with me. I was the one given the policy which I never took time to read. That night, I learned a lesson more valuable than what the Seminar might have taught me had I been able to attend: authenticity can transform contention into closeness. My son pretended he didn't care about the pain he saw in my face when in reality he really did. My son could have kept quiet forever and pretended like it didn't matter to him how disappointed I was. Instead, he shared what was true for him: that he too was in pain and disappointed for me. I learned that his annoying behavior is not who he really is. His authenticity is. That night, he showed me who he truly is: a compassionate, loving, and concerned human being. And, in that space of coming to know him, I felt comfortable, recognized, and peaceful. I felt close to him.

If this was the lesson I was to learn by missing the first day of the ten-week seminar series of The Landmark Forum, then it was a lesson worth learning, and paying over $120 for!

LESSON APPLICATION

What lives in the heart of an individual may be inconsistent with his/her behavior. That which brings consistency – where the heart and behavior match - is authenticity. Authenticity is a quality of the soul. Authenticity is something you are, not something you do. Being authentic means you don't hide and you don't pretend.

Merriam-Webster defines authentic as "true to one's own personality, spirit, or character." True to one's own spirit is worth further examination.

The spirit of every human being is signed, sealed, and delivered in perfection. There is nothing lacking, and we are whole as spiritual beings. However, we perceive others and ourselves to be just the opposite: incomplete human beings, lacking in so many ways. Nevertheless, we are spiritual beings living a human existence, and all the "humanness" of life weighs down our spirit and keeps it hidden underneath. We then believe we are the flesh and blood that walks, acts, talks, thinks, reasons, etc., when we are much deeper than that. Authentic, then, means being true to one's own Spirit (with a capital "S"), which is our highest Self. Our Spirit longs to live authentically, even while in the human body. Our job is to allow it to come from the shadows and into the light. When we do, we find joy, peace, forgiveness, power to create a life of our own choosing, and good relationships.

With all the gifts authenticity brings, what then, keeps us from being authentic?

One main reason is fear. This fear includes the following:

- not being liked
- rejection
- punishment
- looking bad
- being wrong

And, there is one more biggie...

- ...fear of KNOWING how powerful we really are.

We don't take the time to get to know our Spirit, who we truly are, nor the Spirit of those with whom we are in relationship. We look at what they DO (and judge) rather than who they ARE (and love).

It's hard, isn't it? It's hard to love someone and not judge her when her behavior disturbs, even hurts you, especially when you remain disturbed and hurt for a long time. However, if you really want to have power, freedom, and self-expression with yourself and in your relationships with others, you can.

Here are some steps to be authentic in relationships:

1. Start with self-examination by asking yourself, "What am I pretending and what do I really feel/want?" For example, are you pretending you don't need love from someone in your life when you really do? Are you pretending you are always right when sometimes you are wrong? Make a list of three specfic areas where you are pretending. You will have to acknowledge the temptation to start with how others may pretend rather than how you pretend. When you start with yourself, you will find it easier to be authentic with others. The goal here is to recognize where YOU (not your lover, mother, sister, brother) have been inauthentic.

2. Look at these three areas again. Make a decision to accept yourself just as you are, understanding that as a Spirit being, you are whole and complete, lacking nothing. You may want to criticize yourself for these areas of inauthenticity, but don't. You also may be tempted to justify yourself, but don't.

3. Choose one of those three areas and share it with someone who is NOT CONNECTED to this area. Ask the person you shared this with if s/he felt moved, touched or inspired by what you shared. If yes, you are on the right track. If no, you haven't gotten real

just yet (if no goose-pimples show, try again). Think again about what you are pretending and come back and share. The goal is to get comfortable with being authentic and experience what it "feels" like to others.

4. When you are comfortable with one area, move to a second. The goal here is to recognize where you are being inauthentic and to become comfortable with living authentically in all areas of your life. Don't worry if you can only address one area and three seems overwhelming. Start with where you are.

5. Choose one of those three areas and share it with someone who IS CONNECTED to this area. The goal here is to transform distance in a relationship to closeness.

YOUR TURN

Think about a relationship where you feel distant from the other person, someone with whom you'd like to feel closer. Write down an area in which YOU have been pretending and the manner in which you have been pretending. Then, write down what you really feel/want. Remember, while you may want to write about what he/she didn't do, doesn't do, etc., this other-focus will perpetuate the distance you feel. Closeness will come when you get real with the other person about what YOU (not they) have been pretending. Re-read what you have written. If you feel moved, touched, or inspired by what you wrote, (goose-pimples) the person who will hear it will likely feel the same (but don't demand that they respond accordingly!). If you don't feel moved, touched, or inspired by what you wrote, neither will the other person. Keep writing and re-writing until you truly feel it.

_____

_____

"Once you find deep solitude and calm, there will be a great gladness in your heart. . . . There will be bliss, wonder, the awe of attaining something pure and sacred."

- Deng Ming-Dao

LESSON

11

Don't Wake And Run. Wake And Wait!

It was the same stressful routine day after day, every single morning:

- Alarm goes off around 6 a.m.
- Hit snooze button two, three, four more times
- After fourth time, realize I overslept
- Jump out of bed and frantically wake my kids
- Get kids dressed (or scream at them to dress themselves)
- Make sure homework, paperwork, school work are placed in backpacks
- Cook breakfast
- Eat quickly
- Rush out front door while screaming, "Hurry UP, or we are going to be late!"
- Buckle seatbelts/attach booster seats
- Drive to school
- Park and unbuckle seatbelts/ detach booster seats
- Escort each child to respective classroom
- Kiss each good-bye

- Jump back in car; head home
- Park in drive way
- Head back inside house
- Clean-up
- Head back to school for noon pick-up
- Pick-up youngest
- Three hours later, pick up others
- Head back inside house
- Start homework and give snacks
- Prepare for dinner
- Eat dinner
- Prepare for baths
- Read stories
- Tuck each into bed
- Lights out
- Next morning, Repeat

Morning after morning, this was the routine. The routine changed a bit when I worked full-time, but the frenetic pace didn't.

I couldn't stand this routine. It depleted me, sucking the very life out of me. I remember talking aloud to myself, saying, "There HAS to be a better way. This is not working. There has to be a better way." In my mind, a better way could have been any or all of the following: 1) a nanny (full-time, of course); 2) a cook; 3) a maid; 4) a driver; 5) a calm, cool, and collected clone of myself.

A better way presented itself, but not in any of the forms above. It happened one day while watching the Oprah Winfrey show. Her show was about meditation, more specifically, a form of meditation that she began to practice, along with her employees. I had never heard of this particular form, though I was familiar with mediation, in the generic sense. Her show was about a form of meditation called Transcendental Meditation (TM). It sounded "new age" to me, but I was intrigued nevertheless. Most intriguing was the description of health benefits that Transcendental Meditation[29] can confer. As someone who is interested in health and well-being, I listened carefully to the impressive list of benefits, including: stress relief, reduced blood pressure, slowing of the aging process, increased productivity, increased creativity, and increased intelligence. These were just some of the many benefits. Oprah shared highlights of her visit to Fairfield, IA -- the mecca of Transcendental Meditation in the United States. While my eyes were glued to Oprah's televised trip to Fairfield, IA, I too decided that I wanted to make the same pilgrimage and perhaps learn the practice of Transcendental Meditation. Nearly two years later, I found myself aboard a plane heading for...you guessed it: Fairfield, IA.

I arranged to stay at the Raj Resort for a women's retreat called, "Awaken." Upon my arrival into Des Moines, IA, a woman driving an old, beat-up van waited for me outside the airport. Would this be the way I would start my memorable trip to Fairfield? In an old, beat-up van? The van was so old that I began to doubt it would make the two-hour trip from Des Moines to Fairfield. I was a bit worried; however, the driver had a warm, assuring, and friendly personality. She calmed my fears as she explained that her van, while run-down in appearance, was internally in good shape. During our two-hour trek, she informed me that she has been practicing Transcendental Meditation for over 20 years! Wow! In fact, Fairfield has been referred to as "the world's largest training center" for practitioners of the Transcendental Meditation technique.

As we entered the city limits of Fairfield, an unexplainable sensation took over my body, both unexpectedly and immediately. The sensation made me feel as if I had just taken a sleeping pill, a sensation of total relaxation and peacefulness. I mentioned this sudden sensation to my kind driver, and she offered an explanation: "That's the universal effect of Transcendental Meditation from many practitioners in one place. Group practice of Transcendental Meditation brings about calm and peace, even world peace." It sounded a bit far-fetched, until she cited a study conducted in Washington, D.C., that demonstrates the correlation between Transcendental Meditation and the reduction of violent crime. Based on the results of the study, the steady state gain (long-term effect) associated with a group of 4,000 participants in the Transcendental Meditation pilot was calculated as a 48% reduction in violent crimes in the District of Columbia.[30]

My kindhearted driver dropped me off at the Raj Resort. Our conversation had been so informative and enlightening for me, that I knew my time in Fairfield would be more of the same. For four days, I was immersed in learning and practicing Transcendental Meditation. I was paired with a Transcendental Meditation teacher, whom I will never forget. My teacher guided me in the practice and taught me my personal mantra ('mantra' is a sanskrit word meaning 'tool of the mind'--it is a sound that has specific known effects.' The mantras used in the TM technique allow the mind to settle down while the body relaxes and they have a life-supporting effect on the nervous system.). Once an individual receives a mantra, he/she is instructed to keep it private. The new practitioner is asked to keep private everything that is learned in private. The TM technique led me into a world of calm, peace, and wisdom that I knew had to exist, but I had no idea where. That place does exist, and it is within me. Calm, peace, and wisdom patiently waited for me to discover that they had always been there, and that they had always been my constant companion and forever will be. They only ask that I take time out of the busyness of my daily routine to welcome their presence.

My daily tasks have not changed substantially since my time in Fairfield. What has changed, however, is how I begin and end each day now. Every morning and every late afternoon, I set my timer for 20 minutes on a soft alert. Sitting comfortably in my bed or a chair, I close my eyes. In those 20 minutes as I do the technique, my mind becomes quiet. In that quietness, calm, peace, and wisdom arise. I shared with my children both my experience while in Fairfield and my experience learning the practice of TM. When I first began to practice TM, my children often interrupted me by knocking and banging on my door. Once I explained to them how important it was for mommy to meditate, how calm it makes her feel, and that she is in a better mood to play and chat, they discontinued interrupting me. Daughter 3 made a sign for me that I hang outside my door that reads, "Meditating. DO NOT DISTURB." She drew a cute picture that goes with it.

Often during meditation, I experience deep rest, rest that is deeper than sleeping. My mind is also restful but wakeful at the same time. I repeat my 20 minutes of meditation in the afternoon, before my children come home from school. Now, my body has become so accustomed to the meditation experience that it alerts me when I am late for a session. When I am late for a session, my mind becomes foggy and my body becomes tired. It's equivalent to hunger pangs. When I miss a meal or am late eating one, my body sends my brain signals that it is time to eat. As soon as I am done meditating, my mind becomes alert and my body becomes refreshed. In fact, my children can tell when I have missed my meditation. When I get cranky, they ask, "Mom, did you meditate today?" And usually the answer is, "Not yet, but I will now."

I have been practicing the Transcendental Meditation technique faithfully for two years. When I awake in the morning, I no longer jump out of bed and haphazardly run around completing those mind-numbing tasks listed early. I sit and meditate and my true inner Self awakens within. I wait for my inner voice to impart wisdom into my day, my concerns, and my plans. I remain still in the calm, peace, and wisdom that meditation offers.

Now, my days of "wake and run" are replaced with, "wake and wait."

LESSON APPLICATION

The official website for Transcendental Meditation best explains what Transcendental Meditation is:

Transcendental Meditation is a simple, natural, effortless procedure practiced for 20 minutes, twice each day, while sitting comfortably with the eyes closed. It's not a religion, philosophy, or lifestyle. It's the most widely practiced, most researched, and most effective method of self-development.

The Transcendental Meditation technique allows your mind to settle inward beyond thought to experience the source of thought — pure awareness, also known as transcendental consciousness. This is the most silent and peaceful level of consciousness — your innermost Self. In this state of restful alertness, your brain functions with significantly greater coherence and your body gains deep rest.

More than five million people worldwide have learned this simple, natural technique — people of all ages, cultures, and religions.

Over 350 research studies have been conducted at more than 250 universities and medical schools (including Harvard, UCLA, and Stanford). These studies have been published and peer-reviewed in more than 100 scientific journals[31].

Most mothers start each day in a rush. As soon as our alarm clocks sound (whether internal or external), we hit the ground running. We run to prepare breakfast, get kids dressed and off to school, manage our finances, check social media, wash the dishes, and then go to work (whether at home or in an office).

A study done by the Pew Charitable Trust found the following from its 2005 survey[32]:

Working mothers feel rushed. When asked how they felt about their time, 24% of the public said they always feel rushed. But working mothers' lives are much more harried than the average American's. Four-in-ten working mothers with children under age 18 said they always feel rushed, and another 52% said they sometimes feel rushed. Whether mothers worked part time or full time didn't make a difference: 41% of moms who work full time and 40% of those who work part time said they constantly feel rushed.

It's difficult to find ten minutes for yourself each day, isn't it? How then will you ever find 20 minutes, twice a day, to meditate? I know it seems like a luxury, but it is not. Actually, it is a necessity. Consider what Transcendental Meditation does for mothers, which is stated directly from the Transcendental Mediation website for women[33]:

Meditating Moms
Moms need meditation probably more than anyone does. We'd like to think we'll be able to ignore our needs while taking care of children, work and home. But children are sensitive to a mother's stress and reportedly have higher stress themselves when the mother is overworked, anxious or depressed. With so little time to spare for meditation, moms need a practice that works and doesn't require

clearing their busy mind of thoughts or having to concentrate or focus.

A powerful stress-buster for moms

The Transcendental Meditation technique is easy to learn and effortless to practice, and most importantly it's a powerfully effective stress buster. Research has found that TM practice produces a state of profound relaxation, much deeper than ordinary rest and accompanied by increased alertness and orderly brain function. Regular practice results in decreased anxiety and depression, reduced insomnia and hypertension.

Meditate, and nourish yourself

Intuition, patience, wisdom, love—all the divine qualities associated with motherhood—often depend on how rested we are, how aligned we are with our own inner voice and source of nourishment. By diving deep within during TM practice, the mind effortlessly settles to quieter levels of thinking, transcending the pressures, worries and agitation of the active mind. Twice-daily experience of inner silence, happiness, and energy not only replenishes our depleted reserves but also creates vibrant consciousness and a naturally relaxed, stress-resilient physiology.

Fitting meditation into your busy life

Many mothers find that fitting meditation into their day more than makes up for the time it takes. Whether it's during your baby's nap, after your kids go to school, or before they come home, taking time to nourish yourself prepares you to be 'on' for others. If you work outside the home, meditating first thing in the morning or on your break at work may be best. As a mom, consider bringing meditation to your family. The TM technique can be learned by children as early as age ten, and there is also a technique suitable for children under ten.

I encourage you to learn Transcendental Meditation. If you think, "I can't sit quietly for 20 minutes twice per day...I'm too busy", you are not alone. I thought the same. Yet, my breakdown and breakup necessitated finding a source of deep rest and peacefulness that I had never known before. Your children will experience a calmer mom. Meditation can help you become not only happier but also more productive at home and at work. Isn't this what we all want?

YOUR TURN

Understanding the benefits of meditation, how might your day be more productive and fulfilling if you took time to meditate on a daily basis? What might work that is not working for you now? If you already meditate on a daily basis, how can you become an advocate of this practice so that other mothers can benefit?

_____

_____

_____

_____

_____

_____

_____

_____

_____

_____

_____

_____

_____

_____

_____

_____

_____

_____

> # "When we adore our children, we create the ultimate condition for them to rise."
> *- Pamela Elaine*

LESSON

12

Love Is Not Enough. Adoration Is!

As the youngest of three children, I know my parents loved me and still do. I know they wanted the best for me: to do well in school; to have strong friendships; to become a respectful and respectable woman; to give of my gifts and talents to the world; and to find happiness in loving relationships with others. My parents ensured that my needs and many of my wants were met. They provided me with food, clothes, discipline and correction when necessary, a safe place to live and to lay my head, a good school to attend, and even a car at age 16, which my sister, brother and I shared. My parents were not rich by any stretch of the imagination. What they did have, they shared with their children, generously. I was loved. My brother and sister were loved too.

On the other hand, with all of the security and good intentions of my parents, a fundamental need was never met. I needed to feel deep affection from them. They loved me, as I stated. However, there was little to no sign of deep affection, such as hugs and kisses on a regular basis. Actually, displays of affection were rare. Okay, there were occasional hugs and kisses when something special happened, like graduating from middle and senior high school, getting awards, or doing well in the school play. In other words, I only received hugs and kisses from my parents when I did something to make them proud. However, they rarely hugged and kissed me simply because I existed, because I was their little human creation. In all fairness, I recall times when my mom would rub my cheeks with her hand, as a sign of affection. That was nice and it made me feel so special. I can remember one time I sat on my father's lap and rubbed my soft cheek against his prickly beard. That was nice, and it made me feel special too. I do not recall routine, "no-reason-needed," "because-you-are-special" hugs and kisses.

Curious about the importance of both love and affection in my parents' household, I interviewed my father and mother separately to find out if they experienced signs of love and affection from their parents:

1. During your childhood and your growth into adulthood, did one or both of your parents give you hugs and kisses on a daily basis?

2. Describe the affection that you witnessed between your mother and your father.

3. Did you ever want hugs and kisses from your mother, father, or other caregivers, whether as a child or as an adult?

4. Did you ever receive hugs and kisses from someone, and if so, did you feel that you finally got something you had been missing?

5. If you could turn back the hands of time as a father/mother with your own young children, what would be your view/attitude/actions toward hugging and kissing your children, and why?

Both of my parents reported that they felt loved by their parents. Neither, however, received hugs and kisses as part of their daily experience. Hugs and kisses were doled out in response to "doing or accomplishing something," such as receiving good grades or graduating from school. Hugs and kisses were not doled out "just because." Neither of my parents witnessed affectionate hugs and kisses between their own parents. When they became adults, they both experienced regular hugs and kisses from the person with whom they fell in love. Ironically, it was with each other. That relationship led to marriage after a very short courtship...and then divorce after more than 30 years.

In turning back the hands of time, both admitted that their views, attitudes, and actions regarding hugging and kissing their children is different now than it was while raising us. Their responses to my last question was the most profound for me, one which brought tears to my eyes as I recorded their answers:

"I would totally, whole-heartedly grab them every day and say, 'I love you,' and we would do things together every day. I wouldn't let my work get in my way. I wouldn't let anyone get in my way. I

would spend the quality time. Individually, I would give my time and attention based on their individual needs. That would be the main thing I would do."

- My mom

"I would show unlimited signs of affection: hugs in the AM and at night, letting them know that 'I love you;' spending the time together; would never depart; would give my life to Jesus; a family led by God; would be heaven on earth."

- My dad

What I found fascinating were the similarities between my parents' lives and my life, more specifically, in my relationships with men. I was a teenager when I had my first real boyfriend. This man loved me AND gave me hugs and kisses regularly. After a very short courtship, we married. I was 18 years old. Four years later, we were divorced. I was an adult when I had my second real boyfriend. This man loved me AND gave me hugs and kisses regularly. After a short courtship, we married. I was 30 years old. Eighteen years later, we were divorced. There was a direct correlation between a decrease in hugs, kisses, and affection within both of my marriages, and an increase in my feelings of insecurity, unhappiness, and tension, and the frustration level between us. I loved these men and they loved me. However, the fewer the hugs and kisses between us, the greater the disconnect became. Love was important, but not enough.

My boyfriends-turned-husbands loved me and touched, held, kissed and gave me endless attention. In other words, they gave me what I craved. Love plus signs of affection from boyfriends compensated for the absence of signs of affection from my parents. I was hungry for signs of affection, mostly from my parents, but if love plus signs of affection had to come by way of boyfriends, then so be it.

I love my kids. I want the best for them--to do well in school, to have strong friendships, to become respectful and respectable individuals, to give of their gifts and talents to the world, and to find happiness in loving relationships with others. Their father and I provide for their needs and many of their wants. They are well fed, and they always have clean, nice clothes. They are disciplined and corrected as necessary, have a warm place to lay their heads, attend a good school, and may one day get a car to share among the four of them. Their father and I are not wealthy by any stretch of the imagination. What we do have, we generously share with our children.

On the other hand, with all of the comfort and good intentions love brought, one basic need went unmet. That need was affection. I did not demonstrate affection toward my children consistently when they were younger. Granted, there was an occasional hug when they picked up their toys or brushed their teeth without being told to do so, or if they won first place in the spelling bee. I hugged and kissed them because of what they "did" (something to make me proud or less stressed). However, I did not demonstrate affection just because of whom they "are" (just because they are my little human beings). When I honestly confronted my personal and painful truth, that being a mother was not what I really wanted, and when I looked back on my upbringing, I realized something: I do not know what deep affection looks or feels like. How can I possibly give something to my children that I have never received for myself? In my opinion, love was a need. It had to be met. Affection was not. It was a luxury.

As a mother, I fell into the default behavior of giving to my children what I got from my parents: love without affection. Rather than coupling my love with hugs and kisses, I gave them speeches on the merits of completing tasks perfectly and offered correction whenever they failed to do so. My children HAD to complete a task almost perfectly; otherwise, they received criticism and correction from me. My mantra was: "Do it right the first time or DO IT OVER." If they did a task well, they were rewarded with praise (not affection, however). If they didn't, they were criticized.

One day I noticed something curiously annoying that occurred each time I asked my oldest, most responsible child to scramble eggs, which she had done on numerous occasions. She asked me at every step if she was doing it correctly: "Mommy, is this the right way to take the eggs out of the refrigerator?" "Is this the right way to crack the egg?" "Mommy, what is the right setting again for the stove top?" "Do you think the eggs are done now, Mommy?" "Should I use a spatula or a spoon to scoop out the eggs?" I became so annoyed with her questions that I asked her point-blank:

"Why ('in the heck') do you keep asking me to show you how to do something that you already know how to do?"

Her response was insightful:

"Because I am afraid."

"Afraid of WHAT?" I demanded.

"Afraid of making a mistake and then you will be mad at me." She confessed.

Afraid of making a mistake and then I will be mad at her? I marveled at her insightfulness. And, I felt terrible too. What message was I conveying to her day-in and day-out by my excessive focus on completing tasks correctly? In that moment I was confused because I thought my parenting style was helping her grow into a responsible and capable child. I was confused because I love her but wondered if she felt my love. And in that same moment, I felt ashamed that my parenting style made her feel that her mistakes equate to the withdrawal of my love. What was I doing to my daughter's self-esteem (and my other children's too)? What about her sense of wholeness? What about her sense of belonging and connection to me? I didn't know, and I was disturbed that I didn't.

Years later, after reflecting on this incident, and asking myself questions about its meaning, I would come to understand. From studying the writings of child psychologists, learning about emotions, and my personal experiences, I would come to learn that while love for my children is definitely necessary, there was something more they needed from me.

LESSON APPLICATION

Love is important, but it's not enough.   The word "love" can be confusing and is too broad. The term is used to express a myriad of experiences: "I love chocolate cake." "I love that dress." "I love that movie." "I love my mother." Is love a feeling or an action? Does it encompass both, along with so much more? Ask ten people what love is and you will hear ten different answers. "What is love" was the most searched phrase according to the company, Google. An acclaimed newspaper and winner of the Pulitzer Prize for public service – "The Guardian[34]" – sought to get to the bottom of the question once and for all. "The Guardian" gathered writers from the fields of science, psychotherapy, literature, religion, and philosophy to give their definition of the broad word, "love."

The theoretical physicist and scientist said that love is basically chemistry. In other words, the brain releases chemicals like oxytocin, norepinephrine, serotonin, vasopressin, and dopamine, which are involved in bonding and attachment. However, love can be viewed as an evolutionary process, meaning a survival tool to promote long-term relationships, support children and enhance feelings of safety and security.

The psychotherapist said there are six types of love that the ancients labeled: 1) Phila, which is non-sexual intimacy; 2) Ludus, which is playful affection; 3) Pragma, which is mature love that develops over time; 4) Agape is love for humanity; 5) Philautia is self-love; and, 6) Eros is sexual passion and desire. The psychotherapist states that while we lump all of these various emotions into one word ("love"), the ancients did not, and instead recognized distinctions. All six types are not likely to be one's experience with the same person, however.

The philosopher said the answer is indefinable or hard to pin down. It is indefinable, he writes, because love is not one thing. Love is many feelings for many different people. However, he believes that love is an innate, passionate commitment that we then nurture and develop over time.

The romantic novelist said love is relative: if you are secure in love, it can feel as necessary as air. If you are deprived of love, it can feel all consuming and as real as a physical pain.

And, the nun said love is an experience found in acts of kindness, generosity towards others, and giving of ourselves, just as God acts towards us. Love, she states, never hurts another, although it may cost dearly. Love cannot be bought or sold.

I wasn't interviewed for my definition; however, this is my opinion about love:

> *Love is important. Love is "always seeking the highest good for another." I learned this definition when I was a teenager attending a spiritual conference for youth. The keynote speaker stated this definition that has remained with me. I found the definition simple, yet profound. Love, according to this speaker, was not a feeling, but an action. Love is a doer. However, love is not enough. Love needs a partner and that partner is deep affection.*

- Pamela Elaine

Love plus deep affection (or action plus feeling) is adoration. Adoration is the sum of the two, making the equation complete, making complete the experience our children need and want with and from us. Adoration is defined as love expressed with **deep** affection, and that expression can include hugs, kisses, touches, etc. The term adoration comes from the Latin adōrātiō, which means, "to give homage or worship to someone or something." One of the best definitions I found for adore is, "To regard with deep, often rapturous love." "Rapturous" is an adjective that means filled with great joy or ecstatic! We associate adoration often with a deity, and rightfully so.

And when we adore or give adoration to a deity we, in effect, give our heart (feelings) to that deity. With a heart of adoration, we are saying to that deity:

- You are important to me.
- Your presence matters.
- You are worthy of my time and attention.
- You are perfect and whole, just as your are.
- You don't need to be fixed, because you are not broken.
- You are unique and there is none other like you.

We do not think of our children as deity. Yet, I believe they are divine creations who come into our lives to make us whole, help us heal, and bring balance, joy, and happiness into our lives. Clinical psychologist and author, Dr. Shefali Tsbary, writes in her book, The Conscious Parent[35],

"The conscious parent understands that this journey has been undertaken, this child has been called forth to raise the parent itself; to show the parent where the parent has yet to grow. This is why we call our children into our lives."

During one of her interviews and her TED (Technology, Entertainment, Design) talk, Dr. Tsbary said:

"Parenting is the coming together of so many different worlds, of so many dualities: it's the nexus of the doing and the being. You gotta do…the doing preoccupies you. But then you realize that in order to meet the spirit of the infant…you have to become into being. So the doing and the being are constantly colliding."

"It's no surprise that we fail to tune into our children's essence. How can we listen to them when so many of us barely listen to ourselves? We have all begun living lives betraying our inner self. We've just divorced ourselves from this notion of wholeness. We believe we are incomplete. And it is this legacy that we keep passing on to our children."

Children ARE a deity, in the sense that they are divine creatures. With a heart of adoration, we are saying to them:

- You are important to me.
- Your presence matters.
- You are worthy of my time and attention.
- You are perfect and whole, just as your are.
- You don't need to be fixed, because you are not broken.
- You are unique and there is no one else like you.

When we adore, we give our heart. And the heart is a powerful mechanism that does more than pump blood through your body. The heart, according to fascinating research conducted by The Institute of Heart Math, generates feelings that directly affect the feelings of another person. In other words, a mother's emotional state influences the emotional state of her child, and this influence can be measured! If you, as mother, are in a joyful, loving, affectionate emotional state towards your child, that state influences the feelings of joy, love, and affection of your child.

Dr. Matt Hertenstein, an experimental psychologist at DePauw University in Indiana, reported that physical touch (hugging and kissing our children) increases the release of the "cuddle hormone" called oxytocin. Oxytocin has many benefits: it makes us feel close to one another, decreases feelings of stress, affects trust behaviors, and promotes feelings of devotion and bonding. Dr. Hertenstein also reported that being touched is plain 'ole pleasant. He compared the feeling from a pleasant touch to the feeling one has when consuming sweet tastes. Sweet tastes activate a region of the brain called the orbital frontal cortex, which is located just above your eyes. This is the same area that responds to sweet tastes, pleasant smells, and pleasant touches.

He says, "A soft touch on the arm makes the orbital frontal cortex light up, just like those other rewarding stimuli. So touch is a very powerful rewarding stimulus – just like your chocolate that you find in your cupboard at home.[36]"

Like Dr. Tsbary says, "I called my children into my life, although I had no idea that was what I was doing. No other human beings have been a mirror to my soul's longing, inviting me to be whole, as my children have." When I was busy in the important work of loving my daughter (doing for her as I did with my other children), I did not show deep affection for her, and intuitively, she knew something was missing. The way she made me aware that she was missing something from me was in her need to feel close to me. Her fear of angering me if she made a mistake while scrambling eggs was her innocent way of saying, "Mommy, I know you love me, yet I need to feel whole from your deep affection too."

I now know what it feels like to be adored. I am adored as a mother, and being adored brings healing. While I needed to be adored by my parents, adoration came from my children. My youngest child teaches me everyday how to adore all of my children, as she adores me. From her, I have become attuned to the intense feelings of deep affection and love, making it possible to reciprocate those feelings to her and my other children. She kisses my hands and my lips, while gushing out words of affection like, "Oh Mommy, I love you so, so much." She fans me when I am having hot flashes. She sits on my lap and wraps her arms around me and hugs long and strong. She sends me text messages with rows and rows of smiley faces and hearts. The weeks when she is not in my custody, she texts or calls me with, "Good morning, Mommy" and "Good night, Mommy" messages. And, she never ceases to say, "You are the best mommy ever!"

In return, I give out far more hugs and kisses now than I ever did when my children were younger. The more I allow them to show me the areas where I need to be made whole (the parts of my soul that need to be healed), the more my affection for them deepens. Today, my children give me hugs and kisses daily and extend their arms, inviting me to return the hugs and kisses. For example, I show my oldest teenage daughter affection when I sit next to her while watching a movie. She shows me deep affection when unexpectedly, she comes behind me and wraps her arms around my waist and squeezes me tightly. My teenage son (too cool for hugs and kisses) welcomes my affection when I rub his scalp and watch him melt into a state of total relaxation. He shows me his deep affection by calling my name for no apparent reason in a certain amusing way, "MOMMMMMEEEEE." My middle daughter enjoys long hugs and kisses on her forehead. She returns the hugs to me with words of affection, "Mmmm, Mommy, I love you."

Adoration...mmmm, mmmm. It is a delicious and sweet experience. It offers a double benefit: The one adored experiences wholeness, and the one lavishing adoration becomes whole. As such, adoration creates the ultimate condition for both the giver and receiver to heal and to flourish.

YOUR TURN

Have you ever read the poem by written by Kahlil Gibran in the book, The Prophet[37]?

What are your thoughts and experiences regarding adoration? Were you adored as a child? Did you have any idea what adoration was?

_____

_____

_____

_____

_____

_____

_____

_____

_____

_____

_____

_____

_____

_____

_____

_____

_____

_____

_____

"He who has a why to live can bear almost any how"

- Nietzsche

LESSON

13

A Mission For Living Gives Meaning To Life's Messes.

During my senior year of high school, we met. He was the nicest guy I had ever known. He gave me what I felt I was missing from my father: time, attention, interest, affection, and a reason for self-esteem. He and I were part of a gospel group known as "The Chosen Generation." During The Chosen Generation's summer tour to Samoa, Western Samoa, and the Fiji Islands, we fell in love. At the end of the summer, we made the bold decision to marry and began planning a wedding for December of that same year. God was telling us to marry, so we believed. I was 18 and he was 21. He had a steady job as a computer technician and I had...well...a high school diploma and one completed semester at the University of Irvine, California. While at the University, I took three classes, and I received a failing grade in every one of them – mostly because I took courses for which I was neither prepared for nor interested in enough to work hard. Rather than declaring a major that I actually had an interest in and would enjoy, I declared a major that I thought would impress my father: Physics (What was I thinking?)! It was bad enough that there was little I found exciting about the required high school physics course I took. Physics at the University level was 1000 times less exciting. Three months later, I left the distant memory of the University, along with my poor grades, in exchange for marriage at the (im)mature age of 18. We had known each other for little more than one year.

For the first several months of our marriage, we lived with his mother (who was a divorced mother of six children), three of his sisters, and his baby brother. That's right--six family members, who had always lived together, and one outsider -

me. And an outsider is how I certainly felt! I had no job, no skills, no savings, no retirement plan, no car, no home of my own, a mother-in-law who was not terribly fond of me, and clearly, no direction. After three months, I demanded that we move. He found a small, one-bedroom apartment twenty miles north of his mother's home in Los Angeles. There, I played housewife. I agreed to the role in the beginning, but later I found myself miserable doing it. I did not want to be a housewife, although I believed that was expected of me. I really wanted to work in the medical field, but his desire was for me to be a housewife, so a housewife I remained.

I allowed him to control the finances. In fact, I don't think I even knew what type of bank account we had, how much money we had, nor how much our bills totaled. I recall asking for an allowance so I could have money to purchase a few minor things for myself, the most important of which was a bean burrito with green sauce from Taco Bell! Until the time I mustered the courage to ask for an "allowance," my friends would treat me to Taco Bell. One friend in particular would regularly treat me. It became the highlight of my week when Donna would call me to say, "Hey girl, let's go to Taco Bell. Don't worry. I'll treat you!" Wow! Those 45 minutes at Taco Bell with Donna made my broke existence somewhat bearable. Finally, after much begging, complaining, and justifying, my husband agreed to give me an allowance. He granted me a generous $5 per week! Not a lot, but enough to buy a bean burrito with green sauce and a soda for my friend and me.

I lived off of $5 a week only for so long. I wanted more, so I told him I wanted a job. He protested and forbade me to work. After all, his mother raised six children and she never worked. He was not going to have his wife work either. It sounded so cute and so protective, at first. So, I didn't work. Instead, I concentrated on being an obedient housewife, although that certainly didn't make me feel happy or fulfilled. Inevitably, as the months and years passed, the cuteness faded. I decided to be defiant. I went out to get a job anyway. I started off making less than $5 per hour as a medical records filing clerk. It was boring work, but it was my own money nonetheless.

Soon, I wanted even more. I decided to finish my education. I enrolled and took courses at the local community college in hopes of transferring to the local University to pursue a degree in the medical field. My ultimate goal was to provide health for and healing to others. While attending school, I worked at a doctor's office as his medical assistant, where I was rather unskilled. I made many mistakes, including the instance in which I wrote in one woman's chart the word "mold" on her skin when I meant "mole." Dr. Fleischner was none too impressed with my inability to distinguish the two. Each workday, I rode two buses to school, which took one hour, and two more buses to work, which took another hour. During that same time, my marriage began to fall apart. My defiance, coupled with my complaints about what I needed to make me happy and fulfilled began to frustrate and alienate my husband. Although we argued often about that, we argued even more about my insecurities. You see, I feared that he was having an affair; the thought of which tormented me, as I relived the memories of unfaithfulness in my parents' marriage.

One evening, when I returned home after a long day at school and work, he was already in the apartment. As I dropped my school books and lab coat in the bedroom, I noticed that the Classified Ads with the apartment section were open on the floor next to his side of the bed. Circled in black ink were several apartment listings in the area. I didn't understand why, but I took note of it and then forgot about it. Some weeks later, I saw the Classified Ads again with other apartment listings circled. So, I asked him:

"Why do you have apartments circled?"

"Because I'm moving OUT!" he snapped.

Moving out? How could he? Why? This declaration seemed to come out of nowhere. Okay, yes, I threatened him on many occasions that I was leaving him. This is what I learned through watching my parents interact. I learned that when the going gets tough, the weak get out. But, leaving him was not what I really wanted. I was dumbfounded.

We argued more and more. He spent more time away traveling for work and for pleasure. He bought himself a motorcycle and would leave for days. I began to worry even more that he was having an affair, but I could never find proof. In time, evidence of his unhappiness surfaced, forcing me to confront a life that wasn't working.

One afternoon, while making my routine stop to the mailbox, I pulled out a letter from a company called "Do It Yourself Law." "Hmmmm…not quite familiar with this piece of junk mail," I thought. My heart started racing as I opened the letter and read it. "He's divorcing me!" I mumbled to myself. As I read the details with shock and disbelief, my breath left my body and my heart dropped to my knees like a pair of oversized panties. Could this really be happening? After several weeks of crying, stalling, begging for and demanding fairness, I finally agreed to the divorce, but only after our relationship had sunk to its lowest point. This happened during a heated argument, when I spouted off that I would contest his demand for a divorce (similar to an "f-you" attitude). And, like a car crashing into the passenger's side, complete with shattered glass and bruises, he called me a bitch. This gentle, kind man who had never uttered profanity in my presence, called me a bitch.

I was in an emotional, physical, and financial MESS! Somehow, I had to put my broken spirit, destroyed sense of self, and non-existent finances back together. Little did I realize that this seemingly impossible feat was intertwined with the pursuit of my life's purpose, that is, a mission that I didn't even realize already existed within me. Yet, as odd as this may sound, my Mission (capital M) knew I needed Her, and She guided me with gentleness and subtlety.

Despite this mess, I still felt compelled to inspire and heal others. I remember when I first felt this calling. I was a teenager. My dear neighbor, Antoinette, lost her grandfather suddenly to a heart attack. I felt deeply for her and her family. They were an integral part of my family. My mom and her mom were close friends. When Antoinette's grandfather died, I wrote in my diary that I was going to find a way to heal the sick and the hurting, like Antoinette's grandfather. That sad experience tucked itself in my psyche and waited for the invitation to express itself in the form of my Mission. I would later invite my Mission to spring forth, though not explicitly.

After the name-calling incident with my husband, we had our worst and final argument. Late that evening, I packed what few clothes I had and moved out of our apartment. For three months, I lived with a couple that happened to be close friends of ours. In exchange for room and board, I took care of their baby daughter. To exacerbate matters, I was fired from my job as a medical assistant (I guess I should have known how to spell "mole" correctly, you think?) just before I moved out. I began a new job search. Every day, I combed through the job listings looking for suitable work for which I might have a chance for employment. As an unskilled, partially educated African American woman living in the white suburbs of Los Angeles, my options for good-paying work were few and far between. Using the public bus system, I traveled to interviews with multiple companies in hopes of finding something that would allow me to contribute financially to my friends' household and save a little to move to my own place. Despite the numerous interviews I went on, I received zero call-backs. I felt pitiful. I didn't even have enough skills to land a minimum wage job.

I remember walking into one business on Ventura Blvd in Sherman Oaks, CA for an interview as a receptionist. The interviewer reviewed my application, saw I had done a little college, and asked me a few questions about myself. She liked what she heard enough to invite me to the next step – a typing test. I sat at the typewriter, poised to fluidly type 75 words per minute. Instead, I pecked. "Darn, a mistake. Oh, shoot another mistake. Where is 'G' on this dumb a** typewriter? I hate this!" At the sound of the bell's DING, my timed typing test was over. The interviewer took my results to tabulate my typing speed. Although the average speed at the time was 60 words per minute, I typed a whole whopping 22 words! The interviewer looked me in my eyes and said something both profound and prophetic, "Honey, why don't you just go back to school?" Me, go back to school? Okay, let's get real. I live with my friends and their newborn baby. I have no transportation of my own. I have no support system nearby. I have no money and too many credit card bills.

Yet, her advice held wisdom that – in time - would lead me to follow my Mission to provide healing to others.

After a three-month, child-care-for-lodging agreement with my friends, I moved back home with my mom. Shortly before I moved back home, my mom helped me buy a used Nissan to travel from my friends' home to hers. I will never forget the day that I found myself in such emotional turmoil from my broken marriage and my broken state (both emotionally and financially), that I got into my Nissan and drove 25 miles from my friends' home to my mom's. In a crying frenzy and crazed mind-set, I cursed, screamed, and banged on my steering wheel as I drove the 25 miles. I cried out to God to help me--help me deal with the mess I was in: the pain of a broken marriage that caught me completely off-guard, my unexpected unemployment, the embarrassment of having no home to call my own. I drove like a maniac until I turned onto my mom's block on 75th Street, in Los Angeles. This is the familiar street where I spent my childhood and teenage years, until I left at the age of 18 to marry for the first time. Deceptively, nostalgia graced me with her smile before smacking me back to reality. Like a mad woman determined to end her plight, I veered my car off the street and onto mom's freshly cut grass, jammed my car into park, and lurched out, leaving the door wide open and the keys still in the ignition. Once I reached her front door, I banged furiously, demanding that someone open it. My sister did. But she could tell that it wasn't her I was banging for. I ran to my mother's bedroom, where she was reclining comfortably and reviewing some papers. In the culmination of emotional exhaustion, I collapsed to my knees in grief at her bedside. My mom, without skipping a beat, grabbed me and just held me tightly as I cried my eyes out in anger, frustration, and disappointment at the mess I was in. I had nothing to offer her, not even a respectful, "hello." I was broke, broken, and befuddled. She asked nothing of me. No explanation. Little did I know that in the midst of the 25-mile drive to my mom's, I had opened the door for my Mission to guide me and prepare the way for my journey.

I moved back home and lived with my mom for nearly six years. She was an anchor and a crucial source of support. She made living with her easy and enjoyable. We got along well. During that time, my Mission gently began to speak to me by helping me remember my desire to help others. I landed a low-paying receptionist job that was 25 miles from my mom's home in Los Angeles. Daily, I'd make the 50-mile, round-trip commute to and from Decision Data Computer Company. The job was comfortable, and the staff was fun to work with. However, I really wanted to go back to school full time. I took one or two courses each semester at California State University at Northridge. I didn't make enough money as a receptionist to take more than two courses. I was determined to finish school. I had to. I knew finishing school was part of my calling, my Mission.

During a lunch break one day, my best friend, Nicole, came to visit me. We had a nice lunch on a warm summer afternoon. When it was time for her to leave, I expressed my longing to be a full time student, although I couldn't afford it. She made an offer I could not refuse. She said, "Well Pam, let's hold hands and pray together, believing that God will make a way for you to go back to school full time." This was not an unusual offer. Nicole and I had made a practice of holding hands and praying together over the years. In fact, we would write down the reason for our prayer requests and write the date any request was answered. We marveled as we looked back on answered prayers. Nicole prayed for me with such passion and sincerity that one would have thought she was praying for a dying aunt. And she was done. That was it. The heavens didn't open up. The angels didn't sing the Hallelujah chorus, and there was no great sign that confirmed her prayer was even heard.

But it was...

Several months later, while on the phone with my dad, I mentioned that I was studying for a test in Biology, and it was tough. He asked me how school was going in general, as well as my job at Decision Data. I told him all was well, but I really wanted to go back to school full time. Lamenting on the fact that I was in credit card debt and was making minimum wage, I had to keep working. I wanted to finish school and get my bachelor's degree so I could move forward and apply to medical school. My father listened carefully. Then he made me an unexpected offer, which I will never forget and will always appreciate:

> "How about this...How about I pay off all your credit card debt, give you tuition to go back to school full time and give you an allowance to live on."

Okay, I know what you are thinking: "This is too good to be true." Right? It certainly felt that way to me. My dad was not a rich man at all. He wasn't even wealthy or close to being wealthy. However, he had been awarded a sum of money (I was unaware of the amount) from a work-related injury. He was willing to share this award money to support me in accomplishing my goal. Naturally, I was overwhelmed and broke down in tears. Wouldn't you? The interviewer's profound and prophetic words entered the forefront of my mind: "Honey, why don't you just go back to school?" I thought to myself, "I will, and I am, Ms. Lady Interviewer." And then I prepared for the inevitable: "Goodbye Decision Data!"

Although completing my undergraduate degree took eight looooong years, which included having to repeat failed classes, I completed a Bachelor of Arts Degree in Biology, nonetheless. I was proud to accept my degree. Guess who was standing in the wings as I accepted my degree? Yes, my Mission. She applauded me most enthusiastically. I did not see her there, however. The moment I accepted my hard-earned degree into my hands, I felt something I never felt before: Empowered.

I applied to medical schools post graduation, but I did not get accepted into any of them. Disappointed, I decided that instead of pursuing medical school again, I would pursue its first cousin: public health. I applied to only three schools: UCLA, UC Berkeley, and Johns Hopkins. I nervously awaited the letters of rejection, thinking that would be my fate, similar to medical school rejection. In the mail came the first letter from UCLA: Accepted! A week or so later, the second letter came from UC Berkeley: Accepted! The final letter came shortly after the second, which was Johns Hopkins School of Public Health: ACCEPTED!!! What??? No way! Not me!!! My Mission stood once again in the wings of my mind and applauded my accomplishment. How could I choose among these three prestigious institutions? My college friend, Boris, made the choice easy when he laughed at my uncertainty: "Pam, Johns Hopkins is the air above the cream of the crop."

Done! Johns Hopkins, here I come!

I moved from Los Angeles to Baltimore, Maryland for graduate school at the Johns Hopkins School of Public Health. The credentials of a Master of Health Science degree from such a prestigious institution enabled me to hold numerous positions in corporate America, where I was responsible for planning programs that offered health and healing.

Back then, my Mission was not crystal clear, concrete, nor even written down anywhere. My Mission resided in my subconscious. She was an ever-present, inner knowing that manifested in my objectives and goals. Although I didn't have an articulated mission, a mission nonetheless influenced my decisions. Mission was driving my pursuits and shaping my goals. Individuals in my life, unknowingly, supported my Mission: Antoinette and her grandfather, my mom, my dad, the job interviewer, Nicole, Johns Hopkins School of Public Health admissions officer, and Boris.

In 2001, 15 years after the mess of going through my first divorce, I moved my Mission from the subconscious to the conscious when I wrote her down on paper. This writing exercise happened after my mentor and friend, Deborah – an author herself - introduced me to the book, <u>The Path: Creating Your Mission Statement for Work and for Life</u>[38], by Laurie Beth Jones. This book guided me to craft a (crude) mission statement:

> *"To awaken, inspire, and encourage greatness in every woman so that she can live her God-given purpose to her fullest."*

Good start. Over time, the mission evolved:

> *"To teach women strategies to live a happy and fulfilling life."*

Over the years, my mission statement evolved as I learned more and more about myself, learned to listen to my inner voice, and learned to pay attention to my passions. As it evolved, I understood that I was merely tweaking the language of a mission that was already settled: to offer hope and healing to women, particularly mothers.

LESSON APPLICATION

Messes happen. The dictionary defines mess as "a situation or state of affairs that is confused or full of difficulties." If you are living the human experience, messes happen, and sometimes, unexpectedly. Remember failing a class and having to repeat it...during the summer? What about the break-up of your parents when you were young? What about losing a loved one to tragedy or illness? Breaking up with your high school sweetheart...after marrying him? The car accident you never saw coming? Messes are like set-backs on the path to a meaningful life. Messes happen, and the disappointment, sadness, frustration, and even despair that you may feel require external support and internal fortitude to manage.

In his book, The Undefeated Mind[39], Dr. Alex Lickerman writes that when we arm ourselves with a mission, we are able to feel that our life is important no matter what the circumstances we face. What may seem like isolated events (throwing a party for a child, take a hot meal to an elderly relative, allowing a stranger to get in line ahead of you) are actually "a series of interconnected plot points that delineate a coherent narrative." That narrative is our mission.

What is a mission? Before giving a specific definition, in general, a mission is fundamentally about bringing value to others if you intend to be fully human. Being fully human means being happy and living a life of joy! No matter how you word your mission, if its intent is to bring value to others, you will experience happiness and joy. Joy leads to success. Messes or "set-backs" in life will take on meaning and can be viewed in the larger context of a happy and joyous life. In fact, the more value we create for others, the more value we create for ourselves. According to Dr. Lickerman, helping others enhances our self-esteem. Certainly, you can have a mission to destroy and take from others. Certainly, you can have a self-serving mission and live that life to the fullest. History proves this. However, according to Nichiren Buddhism, creating value for others is the key to attaining happiness for ourselves.

One of the great psychologists, Abraham Maslow, believed human needs could be arranged in a hierarchy:

- Basic (physical needs like air, food, shelter, etc.)
- Safety and security
- Companionship and affection

He goes on to write something very interesting. I will change the quote slightly so it is relevant to motherhood:

"Even if all these needs are satisfied, we may still often (if not always) expect that a new discontent and restlessness will soon develop unless the [mother] is doing what [she] is fitted for. A musician must make music, an artist must paint, a writer must write if [she] is to be ultimately at peace with [her]self. What a [mother] can be, [she] must be. This need we call self-actualization."

One of the most important steps to self-actualization is to uncover your reason for being on this earth. The process begins with a mission statement for life.

My favorite exemplary mission-driven woman in history is Esther, from the Old Testament of the Bible (Book of Esther). Esther was the beautiful wife of King Ahasuerus of Persia. She had a carefully kept secret – she was a Jew. One day, Esther's beloved Uncle, Mordecai, stood at the gates of the King's palace and overheard one of the King's men plotting to kill all of the Jews. Mordecai knew that the only hope for salvation for the Jews was his niece, Esther. Esther, however, was reluctant to be the savior of her people, until Mordecai appealed to her with these profound words: "Do not flatter yourself that you shall escape in the King's palace any more than all the other Jews. For if you keep silent at this time, relief and deliverance shall arise for the Jews from elsewhere, but you and your father's house will perish. And who knows but that you have come to the kingdom for such a time as this and for this very occasion?" Esther's mission was clear: to save the Jews from annihilation. What a larger-than-life undertaking! However, as you will read shortly, this is the very nature of a mission: larger-than-life, aka, larger-than-oneself.

Esther called upon her people to fast so that she might have the spiritual support, courage, and perseverance to carry out her mission. From entering the King's chamber without first being summoned (a big no-no!), to planning a feast where the truth about this plot against her people was revealed, Esther's actions and experiences were "interconnected plot points that delineated a coherent narrative." In other words, her actions were connected to reveal a greater purpose that each individual act alone may not reveal. As a wife, she most certainly attended to the daily needs of the King and his kingdom. Yet, she fulfilled her tasks while remaining focused on what she was called to do. In the end, those who sought to destroy the Jews were themselves destroyed. The Jews were saved by her hand. Her mission prevailed!

What is your reason for being? What do you feel moved, touched, and inspired by? What moves, touches, and inspires you is in essence a window to your mission. The standard dictionary defines mission as:

"An allotted or self-imposed duty or task; calling"

Best-selling author Laurie Beth Jones points out in her book, The Path: Creating Your Mission Statement for Work and for Life[40], three simple elements to a good mission statement:

1. It should be no more than a single sentence.
2. It should be easily understood by a twelve year old.
3. It should be able to be recited by memory at gun-point.

Most people would say that they have a mission. They just don't know what it is. Most can tell you WHAT they do (teacher, accountant, doctor, writer, secretary, lawyer) and HOW they do what they do. Few can tell you WHY they do what they do. The "why" is the substance of your purpose or your cause or belief. If they do know what it is, they have never written it down in a concise statement, as Jones points out. Simon Sinek explains this well in his book, <u>Start With Why</u>[41]. Sinek found that the most effective leaders are those who **_start_** with their "WHY" (i.e. mission) and work backwards to the "what" and "how!" Understanding "WHY" is the marrow inside the bone of one's mission. "WHY" is the meaning inside the mission.

Do you know what your mission is? Have you ever written it down in the form of a mission statement? If not, it's time to write.

Your mission statement should have breath and depth to cover who you are, your gifts and talents, your activities, as well as your passions.

Your mission or your calling is not what you try to force it to be, or what your parents, spouse/life partner wants, boss, or even your pastor or spiritual leader wants. What your life is supposed to be about is ultimately between you and your Creator. However, your parents, spouse, and others certainly can point you in the "right" direction of your mission, like Mordecai did for Esther. Clues to your life's mission are found in your core values or core beliefs.

In an effort to start you thinking about your life's mission, or to get you to write it down if you already know it, complete the activity below. <u>The Path</u> makes easy the creation of your mission statement with the questions listed below in the activity. Over the next 10 days, schedule 10 minutes in your calendar to sit down with pen and paper or a tape recorder and answer these questions:

Question 1: What are Your three Action Words?

What three action words best describe either what motivates you or describes how you want to help others? There are hundreds of action words, such as accomplish, communicate, counsel, explore, facilitate, finance, heal, inspire, prepare, reclaim, reduce, safeguard, speak, travel, utilize, volunteer, worship, and write.

Record your three best actions words. For example: **1) inspire, 2) coach, 3) facilitate.**

Question 2: What Is Your Core Belief?

What is your core belief? In other words, what do you stand for? What will you defend, perhaps to the death? What do you fundamentally believe in, no matter the changes in time, fashion, politics, or policies? Is it integrity? Justice? Equality? Greatness? Self-actualization? Salvation? Liberty? Service? Family? Freedom? Faith? Excellence?

Record your core belief in this way: My core belief is (blank) because (why?). For example, "My core belief is **well-being** because it a right of every human being."

Question 3: What/Who Moves, Touches, and Inspires You?

What cause moves you to action? Who do you want to help? Think about these following groups or organizations: challenged populations like the visually impaired; individuals with poor or fixed incomes; those in the criminal justice system. Are you moved by or want to help with health care like hospice, medical research, wellness or nutrition? What about community involvement, such as disaster relief, arts/culture, political change, educational equality or literacy? Are you moved by a need to help women/men/children/families, such as family planning, youth employment, money management? Are you moved by spirituality, work, or environmental matters?

Record your two best groups or organizations this way: "What moves me..." Or, "I want to help..." For example: "I want to help **mothers**."

Now, you are ready to put the answers to these three questions into a mission statement.

"My mission is to:

_____, _____, and _____

(action word 1, action word 2 and action word 3)

_____,

(core belief)

to, for or with

_____,

(what moves you/who you want to help).
Let's put it altogether in this example:

"My mission is to INSPIRE, COACH, and FACILITATE the well-being of mothers."

This is my actual mission statement. It has crystalized over time. This was not the actual mission when I was going through my first divorce. However, when I look back on the desire to pursue medicine, then public health, it all makes sense. When I look back on my desire to finish school so that I could pursue medicine/ public health, it all makes sense. When I look back on the long commute to and from work and to school each day, it definitely all makes sense. In fact, writing this book, and you reading it, is fulfillment of my mission.

Don't worry if your first, second, or nineteenth iteration of your mission statement isn't perfect. Trust me, if you keep thinking, reflecting, and writing, it will crystalize into a perfect form for you. At least write it down (or record it) and re-read it weekly. Schedule in your calendar now a reminder to review your mission statement once a week, at a certain time.

Now, within ten days, write your mission statement and commit to fulfilling it if you aren't already doing so.

YOUR TURN

Let's go back to the story of Esther and her mission. Esther took four clear steps. She: 1) understood her mission; 2) accepted her mission; 3) announced her mission; 4) fulfilled her mission. Consequently, the Jews were not annihilated, but were instead saved.

Who will you "**save**" when you fulfill your mission?

_____

_____

_____

"You have a choice: you can do nothing or respond appropriately. It's not necessary to react."

- Nicole O'Neal

LESSON

14

When Mud Is Thrown In Your Face, Don't Take It Personally.

I was in full-blown mommy-mode. This means I was in a no-nonsense, "get-things-done" momentum: organizing, cooking, cleaning, supervising kids, answering the phone, washing clothes, refereeing arguments, helping with homework. You get it? Full-blown mommy-mode is stressful, and I have little patience or tolerance for kids and interruptions. In fact, I will admit that when in this mode, I'm not the most delightful person to be around. Often, when I am in this mode, it is a cover for deeper issues bothering me (but who the hell cares about the "deeper" stuff when STUFF needs to get done!?).

Many concerns were heavy on my mind that day. I still lived in our marital home, performing my motherly and wifely "duties," yet I knew that in a few months, I would no longer be living there. In a few months, I would be divorced and living somewhere else. Where else, I didn't know. I was uncertain and a tad worried about my future and the future of my children.

The evening was getting away from me, and my tasks, as well as the kids' tasks, were still undone. When I noticed that my son had not done his share of the chores, I became angry. Once again, I repeated my instructions to him to take out the trash and pick up his clothes and shoes. The following day was both trash collection and a school day. My son, in what was his usual fashion, spoke defiantly, and with an attitude (I always bristle when any of my children speak defiantly and have an attitude. Why they do the two together baffles me). The exchange went something like this:

Me - "Son, I've asked you over and over again to take out the trash. Go take out the trash and PICK UP YOUR CLOTHES!"

He – "I can't do that right now. I'm in the middle of finishing my homework."

Me – "From what I can tell, you aren't studying. You are goofing off!"

He (now falling apart and rolling his eyes) – "I was just sharpening my pencil! I'll get to the trash later. You don't have to tell me what to do!!!" His face, arms, legs, and torso contorted as he spat these words at me in decibels that were clearly in the disrespectful range.

I was fuming at this point and couldn't see an end to this back and forth, so I created an end.

Me – "Go OUTSIDE until you can calm down and show some respect when you talk to me. Go!" I took a power stance, pointed my finger towards the backyard and stared at him.

What he said next gave me chills. On his way outside, he turned to me. With as much venom as he could secrete, and with teeth visible, he bit:

"I'm glaaaadddd you and dad are getting a divorce..."

That bite was followed by what felt like a ball of slimy, stinky mud thrown right in my face. This symbolic mud hit the top of my hairline and exploded, dripped down my face, covering my eyes, ears, nose, and lips. It tasted salty and felt like little pellets were inside. The mud was cold, as it dripped from my face, onto my clothes and then the floor. After my son threw his mud in my face, he walked out of the house and into the backyard. My instinct was to call him back in and deal him a tongue lashing along with a punishment of no food or drink for the next year. Certainly, that would be just reward for the winner of "The Worst Thing You Can Say to Your Mother Going Through Divorce Contest!" Then, from nowhere, my mind recalled something I read a few times in the book, The Four Agreements[42], by Don Miguel Ruiz:

> "Don't take anything personally. Nothing others do is because of you. What others say and do is a projection of their own reality, their

own dream. When you are immune to the opinions and actions of others, you won't be the victim of needless suffering."

With mud on my face, I had a choice to make, right then and there: to suffer from the bite and the mud, or to refuse to take either personally. Tick tock. Tick tock. Tick tock. Tick tock. Tick tock. Tick tock. Tick tock. Tick tock. In the space of the tick-tocking, I chose the latter. I watched him open the door and go outside. I went to the kitchen and washed the mud off my face, hands and the floor (figuratively speaking), changed into some clean clothes, and went on about my business. As I continued to busy myself, I thought about how much pain my son must be in to say something so unkind. It was the pain he was in that saddened my heart, not the words he said. I understood that what he said was his way to discharge his own pain and anger (about the divorce, about being told what to do, about being punished), and that I really had nothing to do with it.

When his period of punishment in the backyard ended, I opened the door and allowed him to come back inside. He said nothing, and neither did I. He resumed his chores, silently. I continued to do my tasks, though I was no longer in full-blown mommy-mode. My other children were unaware of our confrontation. They were busy upstairs doing their work. I was relieved that they hadn't heard. I had no plans of telling his father when he came home what our son said to me. I saw no point in that disclosure.

Later that night, when the incident had long passed, I was sitting quietly in the family room. My son came over to me and said the unexpected:

"Mommy. I'm sorry for saying that thing about you and dad." I smiled and accepted his apology. I was relieved too, that I took a position of strength by choosing to view his comment as an expression of how he viewed his own reality; that it had nothing to do with me, personally. He chose his response– not me. That's when it was easy for me to say without reservation: "I forgive you." What an incredible boy I have!

LESSON APPLICATION

Isn't it easy to become personally offended by the negative actions and reactions of others? If someone cuts you off on the road, it's easy to retaliate or become offended and internalize the affront as something specifically aimed at you. However, when you make the choice to ignore someone's negative behavior and conclude that it's not about you, you take a position of power. When you understand and then accept that their actions are theirs (whether or not they own them), that they have challenges to work through (as do you), and that it's really not about you, then you won't take offenses personally.

Initially, you may have hurt feelings when someone says or does something offensive. However, with this new awareness, you can deflect the offense by asking yourself a question: "Will I take this act (response, behavior) as a personal offense?" If you allow yourself a moment to process this question, you will then, in that very moment, create "space" (or an opportunity in time) between that act and your feelings to rethink and redirect your response. Creating that "space" gives you enough room to <u>RESPOND</u> rather than to <u>REACT</u>.

According to their definitions, "react" and "respond" hold slightly similar meaning with an important distinction. React means to act in opposition to a former condition or act. For example, suppose someone calls you a "short-tempered cry-baby," and you get highly offended and smack her across her face. In reaction, you call her a "two-faced sell-out." That's reaction. Respond means to react favorably. For example, suppose someone calls you a "short-tempered cry-baby." Rather than take offense, you respond by saying to her, "Hmmm...let me think about whether that's true or not and get back to you." Then, you walk away.

With emotional maturity, you can take the practice of *responding*, rather than *reacting*, even further. When the opportunity presents itself, you can respond to an offensive act (response, behavior) with kindness. For example, suppose someone calls you a "short-tempered cry-baby." An appropriate response might be, "I can only imagine how my behavior may have frustrated you to say something like that. Will you accept my apology?" That will certainly take the fire out of the offense and you may even resolve matters on the spot. Consider the wisdom in the scripture found in Proverbs 15:1;

"A gentle answer deflects anger, but harsh words make tempers flare."

The next time someone "throws mud in your face," practice the technique below. The more you practice, the better you will become at responding, rather than reacting. Responding will become automatic:

Step 1: Ask yourself a question: "Should I take this act (response, behavior) as a personal offense?"

Step 2: Answer the question: "No, I should not take this act (response, behavior) as a personal offense."

Step 3: Make a declaration of choice: "I choose to *respond* rather than *react*."

Step 4: If possible, respond to the offense with: "I can only imagine how my action (name it) must have offended you for you to say/do _____. Is there anything I can do to _____? Or Please accept my apology."

You won't be the victim of needless suffering when you understand that "nothing others do is because of you. What others say and do is a projection of their own reality, their own dream..." You won't find yourself reacting in a regrettable way when you choose to respond with an open and gentle answer.

YOUR TURN

Remember the incident in which someone threw mud in your face (figuratively speaking) and you had a strong reaction to it? Describe it here. Now, recreate that incident using the steps above. How is your response different from your first reaction?

_____

_____

_____

_____

_____

_____

_____

_____

_____

_____

_____

_____

_____

_____

_____

_____

"Someday I will find my prince, but my Daddy will always be my King."

- Pamela Elaine

BONUS LESSON

You Are Fearfully And Wonderfully Made[43].

No, you aren't crazy. Yes, this is the same as Lesson 1. I return to this lesson because it was my ultimate breakthrough. The breakdown that crippled my heart, mind, and soul was the loss of my relationship with my father and the influence it had on who I became. This lesson is worth revisiting again for a very special purpose.

Writing this book and sharing my life lessons is my way of calling forth the gift within me, the gift of providing hope and healing for mothers. The time has come for me to heal completely from the pain of my experience with my father. There was only one obvious way to achieve this type of complete healing, and that was to share with my father the story of where my breakdown began. Although our relationship has improved greatly over the years, I had never told him what Mommy and I found that day in his apartment. In an effort to enhance my own healing and draw closer to him, I invited my father to offer his own lessons, thoughts, and experiences. Why my father made the choices that deeply hurt and affected me was worth hearing and understanding. His side of the story is just as important as mine.

Although I wrote the Lesson Application in most of the other chapters of this book, this chapter features my DADDY'S response, in his own words, as the Lesson Application. I call this the Bonus Lesson! At least, it is for me. I am honored to share it with you. Thank you, Daddy!

LESSON APPLICATION

"Pamela, I am going to share part of my life history. I hope you can see how it relates to your life.

My mother had me out of wedlock when she was 17. She and my father never married. My mother moved from Dallas, TX to Stockton, California when I was three years old, and I was left to be raised by my grandmother and grandfather. My mother got married.

When I was nine years old, my mother came back to Dallas and took me back with her to Stockton, CA. When I was 11 years old, my grandmother came to Stockton and I returned to Dallas, TX with her. My mother divorced and moved back to Dallas, remarried, but I never stayed with them.

When I became a teenager, a thought came into my mind that, "I had a father, but not a daddy. I had a mother, but not a momma. I allowed Satan to speak into my mind that, 'I was a nobody willing to belong to anybody.' I was looking for someone to show me love and recognition, which I never found because I was blind.

When I met your mother, I knew I had found the love I always wanted and we got married and we had Cheryl, Michael and you. Later, when your mother became a teacher for the Los Angeles School District and made friends with her co-workers, there was a change in our relationship. Your mother had a college degree and I had a high school diploma. When I would be with her at dinners and parties, and when talking with her co-workers, I felt like I was an embarrassment to her by the way I spoke words. I went back into the state of mind that I was a nobody, but this time I didn't want to belong to anybody, I just wanted to die.

I never wanted to leave my wife and children. I just wanted to be a daddy and husband. I wanted to give what I thought I never had – love and protection. I left the family but I did not take from my heart the love I had for my wife and children. I left my heart with them. I told myself before I would take anything from them that would cause a financial hard-ship, I would die on the street as a homeless person. After leaving, I thought life would get better and I would receive someone who would accept me being a somebody, and they would be looking for a friendly and loving relationship. For a while, there was a bright light shining. Later, I lost my job; the friends I had were like snow: they were with me if there was no heat. I began to live as Satan told me and light turned into darkness. I returned to being a nobody.

My life was terminated. It was like a court judge sentencing me to death for the crime of sin. I was placed in the gas chamber and they covered my face. I saw darkness and I fell to sleep. When I woke up I was in my prison cell. I said, 'There must have been a breakdown of the gas chamber.' I saw the prison guard coming to me and I said, 'I'm going to die.' The guard said to me, 'Hey you Nobody, dirty trash. You know you should have died last night but another person took your place. His name is Jesus. He said your Father sent Him to die for you.' The guard opened the prison door and said, 'You are free to go!' To me, it was like opening a birdcage for the bird to fly out, but I didn't fly down towards the earth that took my life, but I flew up to the heavenly Father, Jesus, my God who gave me life. Jesus gave me spiritual light, which casts out Satan who only brings darkness. I am not the man I used to be, but I am a better man than I used to be. God said that I am 'fearfully and wonderfully made'.

The message of hope is to all women, young and old…you are fearfully and wonderfully made. You are already healed but you must speak it and believe it. Believe in yourself. Owning your dreams means having your belief in yourself outweigh your fears. When you are hurt or think you have been, or not loved, ask them [the one who hurt you] 'why?' in a manner that you love them and want to be a help to them. But, if they are evil and don't want you to make contact, cast them out of your life with love. Don't carry trash. You dump the trash or you will find it will be hard to remove.

Resist wanting to be approved by people--relatives or friends. Do not look for favors and to be put on a pedestal. You are above and not beneath. This advice will keep you healed. Whenever [you have] a thought that's not godly, cast it out in the Name of Jesus.

Be encouraged because you have the victory. No weapon formed against you shall prosper. Be a peace-maker, not a heart breaker. Believe in yourself, forgive, let go! Become a motivator. Encourage one another."

- Ernest James Nichols

YOUR TURN

Use the freedom of self-expression to write down what moves you.

_____

_____

_____

_____

_____

_____

_____

_____

_____

_____

_____

_____

Suffocating, tolerating things on my plate
There was a lesson to learn, it's that I'm not gonna break.

- Lyrics from "Muddy High Heels"

FINAL THOUGHTS

I learned a dramatic lesson about resilience as I poured my experience into these pages: "Bending" is the heart of resilience. The definition of resilience is "the ability of something to return to its original shape after it has been pulled, stretched, pressed, bent, etc." Meaning, we don't really break, we just bend!

What have your learned about yourself and the possibility of a life wrapped in healing, happiness, and fulfillment? Your personal path to healing, happiness, and fulfillment may not be clear or easy, but it is possible. All you need is a little courage to take the first step onto your own path. If you do, the God of the Universe will rise to support you. Trust that!

You too have a story to tell and lessons to share. No matter what it takes to self-express, do it! It's worthwhile and many lives will be touched, moved and inspired by your openness.

Just by your commitment to read this book, you have already begun to open up to a life of your choosing.

Expect it.

Look for it.

Welcome it.

What Are Your Top Three Life Lessons?
(Write each as a statement)

Lesson 1:

_____

_____

_____

_____

_____

Lesson 2:

_____

_____

_____

_____

_____

Lesson 3:

_____

_____

_____

_____

_____

Share them with others.
If you want, you can email me and share: Thanks@DFGreatness.com

Thank you for sharing this journey with me.
May your life be filled with joy and beauty!

- Pamela Elaine

APPENDIX

[1] The author's edits to the Biblical passage found in Psalms 139:14: "I praise you, for I am fearfully and wonderfully made. Wonderful are your works; my soul knows it very well." – English Standard Version

[2] https://psychologies.co.uk/tests/what-kind-of-fatherdaughter-relationship-do-you-have.html

[3] Allhoff, Fritz; Nease, Lon; Austin, Michael; Fatherhood - Philosophy for Everyone: The Dao of Daddy; Publishers Wiley-Blackwell March 2011 (This material is reproduced with permission of John Wiley & Sons, Inc.).

[4] Kromberg, Jennifer, Psychology Today; "How Dads Shape Daughters' Relationships"; July 1, 2013, http://www.psychologytoday.com/blog/inside-out/201307/how-dads-shape-daughters-relationships

[5] Shultz, Melissa T., "How To Fix The Damage From A Bad Father/Daughter Relationship; Huffington Post, November 4, 2013; http://www.huffingtonpost.com/melissa-t-shultz/father-daughter-relationship_b_4191146.html. (With gratitude for written permission.)

[6] Clawson, Cynthia; "The Best is Yet to Come" from You Are Welcome Here", 1981, Publisher Triune Music.

[7] Leotti, L.A., et al. (2010) Born to Choose: The Origins and Value of the Need for Control. Trends in Cognitive Science, October; 14(10). (With gratitude for written permission.)

[8] IBID

[9] McDonald's Nutritional Facts, 01-08-2014 http://nutrition.mcdonalds.com/getnutrition/nutritionfacts.pdf

[10] 2,000 is standard daily caloric intake for an adult. Your daily values may be higher or lower depending on your caloric needs.

[11] Health and Human Services of the Federal Government recommends no more than 65g fat intake per day, based on 2,000 calorie diet (http://healthfinder.gov/FindServices/SearchContext.aspx?topic=944)

[12] The American Heart Association recommends a daily intake of

1,500mg or less of sodium (that's less than ¾ teaspoon of salt): (http://www.heart.org/HEARTORG/Conditions/HighBloodPressure/

PreventionTreatmentofHighBloodPressure/Shaking-the-Salt-Habit_UCM_303241_Article.jsp)

[13] Hamady, Jennifer, "The Art of Surrender", Psychology Today, July 8, 2013. (With gratitude for written permission.)

[14] Coehlo, Paulo, The Alchemist, HarperOne; 25 Anv edition, April 15, 2014

[15] Seltzer, Leon, "Couples-Stop Fighting Over Money", Psychology Today, November 9, 2012. (With gratitude for written permission.)

[16] "The Straight Facts on Women in Poverty"; By Alexandra Cawthorne, October 8, 2008; The Center for American Progress,

[17] 10th Annual Mom Salary Survey, www.Salary.com.

[18] Tessina, Tina B, How To Be A Couple And Still Be Free, Publisher Career Press; 3rd edition; March 1, 2002. (With gratitude for written permission.)

[19] www.nationalmarriageproject.org

[20] http://www.doctoroz.com/videos/post-divorce-discounts-plastic-surgery-pt-3

[21] Merriam-Webster dictionary

[22] Results vary. You may or may not experience the same results on the same program.

[23] www.Discovery.com

[24] Northrup, Christiane, The Power of Joy: How The Deliberate Pursuit Of Pleasure Can Heal Your Life, 2008, Publisher Hay House, Inc., Carlsbad, CA. (Quoted with permission from The Power of Joy, by Christiane Northrup, M.D., ob/gyn physician and author of the New York Times bestsellers: Women's Bodies, Women's Wisdom and The Wisdom of Menopause; www.drnorthrup.com).

[25] A hormone that is naturally made by the human body. DHEA is used for slowing or reversing aging, improving thinking skills in older people, and

slowing the progress of Alzheimer's disease. (visit http://www.nlm.nih.gov/medlineplus for more information)

[26] www.NSF.gov

[27] Marano, Hara Estroff; "Depression Doing the Thinking: Take Action Right Now to Convert Negative to Positive Thinking", Psychology Today, July 01, 2001. (With gratitude for written permission.)

[28] The Secret on CD, Rhonda Byrne, Simon & Schuster Audio 2006. (With gratitude for written permission.)

[29] www.tm-women.org; 800 635 7173. Transcendental Meditation, Maharishi Foundation USA, 2014. (With gratitude for written permission.)

[30] Hagelin, Johns S. et al, "Effects of Group Practice of the Transcendental Meditation Program on Preventing Violent Crime in Washington, DC: Results of the National Demonstration Project, June-July 1993"; Institute of Science, Technology and Public Policy;

[31] www.tm-women.org; 800 635 7173. Transcendental Meditation, Maharishi Foundation USA, 2014. (With gratitude for written permission.)

[32] Pew Research Social & Demographic Trends, Pew Research Center, Washington, D.C., "The Harried Life of The Working Mother." October 1, 2009; http://www.pewsocialtrends.org/2009/10/01/the-harried-life-of-the-working-mother/

[33] www.tm-women.org; 800 635 7173. Transcendental Meditation, Maharishi Foundation USA, 2014. (With gratitude for written permission.)

[34] "What is love? Five theories on the greatest emotion of all." The Guardian, December 13, 2012, The Guardian News and Media Limited.

[35] Tsbary, Shefali; The Conscious Parent: Transforming Ourselves, Empowering Our Children, Namaste Publishing, November 1, 2010. (With gratitude for written permission.)

[36] Hertenstein, Matt; "The Communication of Emotion via Touch", Emotion, 2009 Aug;9(4):566-73. (With gratitude for written permission.)

[37] Gibran, Kahlil; The Prophet, Publisher Alfred A. Knopf, September 23, 1923.

[38] Jones, Laurie Beth; The Path: Creating your Mission Statement for Work and for Life; Publisher Hyperion, August 12, 1998. (With gratitude for written permission.)

[39] Lickerman, Alex; The Undefeated Mind: On the Science of Constructing an Indestructible Self; Publisher HCI; 1 edition, November 6, 2012. (With gratitude for written permission.)

[40] Jones, Laurie Beth; The Path: Creating your Mission Statement for Work and for Life; Publisher Hyperion, August 12, 1998. (With gratitude for written permission.)

[41] Sinek, Simon; Start with Why: How Great Leaders Inspire Everyone to Action; Portfolio Trade, Reprint edition (December 27, 2011)

[42] From the book The Four Agreements © 1997, Miguel Angel Ruiz, M.D. Reprinted by permission of Amber-Allen Publishing, Inc. San Rafael, CA www.amberallen. com All rights reserved.

[43] The author's edits to the Biblical passage found in Psalms 139:14: "I praise you, for I am fearfully and wonderfully made. Wonderful are your works; my soul knows it very well." – English Standard Version

Grateful acknowledgment is made for permission to reprint opening quotes for chapter lessons by the following:

Lesson 6 opening quote: From THE FIRES OF HEAVEN © 1993 by Robert Jordan. Reprinted by permission of Tor Books. All rights reserved.